Other titles in this series

LONDON'S STRANGEST TALES

EXTRAORDINARY BUT *TRUE* STORIES FROM OVER A THOUSAND YEARS OF LONDON'S HISTORY

TOM QUINN

PORTICO

This edition published in 2012 by
Portico
10 Southcombe Street
London
W14 0RA

An imprint of Anova Books Company Ltd.

ISBN 978-1-907554-64-3

A CIP catalogue record for this book is available from the British Library.

10 9 8 7 6 5 4 3 2 1

Printed and bound by Toppan Leefung Printing, China

This book can be ordered direct from the publisher at
www.anovabooks.com

First published in the United Kingdom in 2008

All pictures: Anova Image Library

D.A.Q. 1958–1981.

Thanks to Charlotte Wadham for advice and inspiration,
to Katy, Alex and James for entertainment and to Barbara Phelan and
Malcolm Croft at Robson Books for encouragement and jolly emails.

CONTENTS

INTRODUCTION

Like all ancient cities, London is an extraordinarily rich source of strange tales. From stories of one-legged escalator testers and unsolved murders to flying rivers, moving churches and human lavatories.

Then there are the tales of extraordinary London characters, oddballs and inventors, mavericks and madmen – like Stanley Green, who spent his life campaigning against peanut eating, or Walter Rothschild, who taught two zebras to pull his carriage down The Mall. And away from people and places, there are the ancient rules and systems of governance that have survived the centuries to baffle historians and create numerous bizarre anomalies – dusty traditions, archaic practices and ceremonies are kept on despite, on the face of it, no longer being necessary.

Bags of nails are still paid for long-vanished plots of land, medieval legacies are still honoured each year and the pursuivants at the College of Arms still initiate prosecutions against those who infringe the rules governing the use of gules, azure and archant.

London's wealth of bizarre tales can be attributed to the city's love of the old ways, which is why much that is odd and ancient in London's social and business life survives. In the City proper, for example, an ancient ordinance defines a road as a highway without houses – which is why, to this day, no thoroughfare in the city may be called a road; it's either a street or an alley. Even big multinational corporations haven't been able to change that.

Many of London's strangest and quirkiest tales are well known to scholars but have been unavailable to the general public until now.

This book is the result of several years spent digging in obscure and dusty archives and in the libraries of organisations whose continued existence in the modern world is itself astonishing, but the labour has been worth it, for whatever your interest, whether political, social, architectural or historical, you will find *London's Strangest Tales* a mighty feast of the mad, bad, dotty, eccentric and – at times – quite unbelievable.

WHY PART OF SCOTLAND IS IN LONDON

950

Scotland Yard is famous throughout the world but few people wonder why a police station in central London should have been given this curious name. Why Scotland? The answer takes us into one of those curious and inexplicable areas of long forgotten history.

From the late tenth century until the Act of Union of 1707 which brought Scotland and England together under one Crown, Scotland was an entirely separate country with its own tradition, rules and statutes – even today Scottish law differs markedly from English law in many respects.

During the period of independence Scotland, like most foreign countries, had a London embassy and the name Great Scotland Yard is the last echo of an independent Scotland's presence in London.

Originally there were three streets that covered this area – Little Scotland Yard and Middle Scotland Yard have long gone – but bizarrely the rules that apply to foreign embassies today still, in theory, apply to this small area of London. All embassies are in practice foreign territory – the police cannot enter a foreign embassy unless invited to do so and their jurisdiction doesn't include the territory of a foreign embassy.

After the Act of Union no one remembered to abolish the foreign status of Great Scotland Yard, which means that even today the little street running off Whitehall near Trafalgar Square is actually Scottish territory.

PUT OUT YOUR FIRE

1066

Many delightful traditions linger in London long after their practical usefulness has gone. The beadle who watches Burlington Arcade, for example, forbids running, umbrellas and whistling despite the fact that these are no longer evidence of a lack of gentility. In parliament an MP under certain circumstances may only interrupt a debate if he first dons a top hat. Ravens are still kept at the Tower of London for fear that if they depart the monarchy will fall.

But perhaps the oddest and longest lasting tradition is the curfew bell still rung each evening in South Square in Gray's Inn, a centre of the legal profession since 1370.

The curfew bell rung here would have been only one of dozens rung all over medieval London, for the word curfew comes from the Norman French *couvre le feu* – meaning put out your fire – and it was rung not to tell citizens that they must not leave their houses but rather to tell them (since it was bedtime) that they should make sure they had extinguished all their fires and candles. The fear – to be realised in the terrible fire of 1666 – was that without a reminder someone might forget a candle or fire and the result would be that the thousands of dry timber and thatch buildings would ignite.

Originally, apart from the bells rung here at Gray's Inn, all London churches rang the curfew – it was on the order of William the Conqueror (1028–87) – and as late as the beginning of the Second World War a dozen or more city churches still rang the curfew. Today that thousand-year tradition is still held in two places – Gray's Inn, as we have seen, and the Tower of London.

THE BISHOP OF WINCHESTER'S GEESE

1171

To those of a religious cast of mind it may come as a shock to discover that for centuries the Christian church made a very good living from prostitution. As it happens the Church was also one of the world's most important and vicious slave owners.

But the church in London was particularly keen to make money from prostitutes since it was so easy – in fact the prostitutes of Southwark were known as the Bishop of Winchester's geese. With magnificent hypocrisy the Bishop of Winchester was able to collect rents from the numerous brothels he owned but then when a prostitute died in the diocese the church refused to allow her to be buried in consecrated ground.

A sad little reminder of this grim and astonishing history can still be glimpsed down a quiet street in Southwark even today. Red Cross Way runs parallel to Borough High Street and if you follow it almost as far as the junction with Union Street you come to a rusty iron gate and behind it a plot of land.

This is the remnant of Cross Bones Graveyard where the Bishop of Winchester's geese were buried when they could no longer earn money for the church.

A royal ordinance of 1171 allowed the Bishop of Winchester to license the brothels, or stews as they were known, and to collect the income. The Bishop's jurisdiction covered what was known as the

Liberty of the Clink – the reference is to the Clink Prison, part of which can still be seen in the Anchor Inn a few hundred yards along the riverbank west from Southwark Cathedral.

In 1833 a history of the area mentions the 'unconsecrated burial ground known as the Cross Bones at the corner of Redcross Street, formerly called the Single Woman's burial ground…'. The writer is clearly echoing the words of a much earlier author, John Stow (1525–1605), whose great *Survey of London* was published in 1598.

Stow refers to Cross Bones and 'these single women who were forbidden the rites of the church, so long as they continued that sinful life, and were excluded from Christian burial, if they were not reconciled before their death. And therefore there was a plot of ground called the Single Woman's Churchyard, appointed for them far from the parish church.'

The brothels, drinking houses, bear-pits and cock-pits of Southwark survived until the death of Charles I on the scaffold in 1649 and the arrival of Oliver Cromwell and a Puritan-dominated government, but when the prostitutes – or most of them – departed, the poor arrived in their droves and by the middle of the nineteenth century this was one of the foulest and most overcrowded parts of London. It was also dangerous – so dangerous in fact that even the police were reluctant to stray too far into its warren of filthy, rat-infested streets and alleys. Cross Bones Graveyard continued to be used until 1853 when the bodies were being buried so close to the surface that decaying hands and feet were often seen sticking through the soil. The government insisted it be closed.

But if proof were needed that the patch of ground that remains really was a burial ground for the Southwark geese, an excavation in 1990 discovered almost 150 skeletons, mostly women and one with the clear marks of syphilis.

With typical greed the authorities have tried again and again to build on the remaining plot of land but fierce local opposition has ensured that, at least for the time being, the old graveyard of Southwark's geese remains as a monument to a long-vanished part of London's medieval history.

HUMAN LAVATORY

1190

As successive British governments have closed Britain's once great wealth of public lavatories – London's loos, until the 1950s, were famous the world over – so has the public been forced to dash in and out of restaurants and pubs where they have no intention either of eating or drinking.

The reason London's magnificent Victorian public loos were built in the first place was simply that governments of the time saw them as essential to the wellbeing of Londoners. Parliamentarians who knew their history far better than today's legislators no doubt remembered that right through the Middle Ages and well into the seventeenth century one of London's biggest problems was the lack of public loos.

In their houses people simply used a bucket or pot and then threw the contents into the gutter or the Thames. There is much evidence to suggest that many householders – this was certainly true in aristocratic households – simply relieved themselves in the corner of any room they happened to be in.

Out in the streets people relieved themselves wherever they liked, but the more delicate-minded and, of course, women found this unacceptable – the solution was provided by human loos.

These were men and women who wore voluminous black capes and carried a bucket. When you needed the loo you looked for the nearest man or woman with a cape and bucket and gave them a farthing. You then sat on the bucket while they stood above you still wearing the cape but also surrounding you with it.

The name of only one human lavatory has come down to us – the court rolls reveal that in 1190 one Thomas Butcher of Cheapside was fined 'and admonished' for overcharging his clients.

THE RIGHT TO BE HANGED BY SILK

1237

The first freedom of the city of London was given in 1237. In late medieval England being granted the freedom of the city was not a courtesy title nor a simple invitation to wander the city at will. Instead it had enormous practical importance. Once granted it meant the recipient was freed from his duty to his feudal lord – he was a free agent and under the terms of the granting of freedom it meant he could own land and earn money in his own right. He was also protected from feudal duties – the duty of military service for example – because he had rights under the charter of the city. These rights were so important that they could occasionally conflict with the rights of the monarch.

The city authorities were careful, however, to ensure that so far as possible the monarch was central to the granting of freedom. The freedom of the city is still granted today and those accepting it have to swear the following oath:

I do solemnly swear that I will be good and true to our Sovereign; that I will be obedient to the Mayor of this City; that I will maintain the Franchises and Customs thereof, and will keep this City harmless, in that which is in me; that I will also keep the Queen's Peace in my own person; that I will know no Gatherings nor Conspiracies made against the Queen's Peace, but I will warn the Mayor thereof, or hinder it to my power; and that all these points and articles I will well and truly keep, according to the Laws and Customs of this City, to my power.

Once he agreed to this the freeman was given a parchment and a wooden casket in which to keep it – in medieval times it is believed that many freemen refused to leave their houses without taking with them – rather like a modern passport – the parchment that confirmed their status as freemen.

Some of the rights granted to freemen are bizarre by any standards – even today a freeman is entitled to herd sheep over London Bridge, he may walk about the city with a drawn sword, can insist on being married in St Paul's Cathedral, is permitted to be drunk and disorderly without fear of arrest and best of all if he is sentenced to hang the execution can only be carried out using a silken rope!

HOW BEDLAM GOT ITS NAME

1250

The grand building that now houses the Imperial War Museum south of the River Thames in Lambeth was once Bethlehem Hospital – the hospital from which we derive the word Bedlam, meaning a state of complete chaos.

The first Bethlehem hospital was built just outside the old city walls near Bishopsgate in 1250. It was then the priory of St Mary of Bethlehem and like all religious houses in Catholic England it had a duty to help the poor and needy.

By the middle of the fourteenth century the records reveal that the priory had been greatly expanded: the new parts of the abbey were specifically designed to house the 'weak of mind', many of whom would have been thrown out of their homes and left destitute.

Early attitudes to the mentally ill were, by modern standards, appalling – if they weren't killed for being possessed by the devil, they were often shackled or kept permanently chained to a wall; they were never washed and often fed, if they were fed at all, like animals; therapy consisted of ducking in freezing water or whipping.

After the Dissolution of the Monasteries, in 1534–41 the whole of the priory buildings of St Mary of Bethlehem became a hospital specifically required to take those who had 'entirely lost their wits and God's great gift of reasoning, the whiche only distinguisheth us from the beast'.

In the late seventeenth century the hospital moved again – this time to open fields just outside Moorgate to the north of the city.

By the mid-eighteenth century, every weekend hundreds arrived to be shown around Bedlam; a visit 'guaranteed to amuse and lift the spirits'.

Designed by Robert Hooke (1635–1703), the beautiful new classical building concealed a dreadful regime, with patients packed into insufficient space and no attempt of any kind at hygiene.

By this time a curious shift had taken place in social attitudes and the entertainment-hungry populace of London began to see Bethlehem Royal Hospital as a sort of circus or amusement park. We don't know exactly when it began but by the mid-eighteenth century every weekend hundreds arrived to be shown around the madhouse; it was a visit 'guaranteed to amuse and lift the spirits', said one commentator.

Sadly there is evidence that the warders deliberately worked the patients up before these visits in order to make them behave even more wildly than they would otherwise. The governors were probably pleased as they had no thought that their patients could ever recover and the visitors paid good money to see them.

By now the hospital was known as Bedlam and the word quickly became synonymous with any scene of chaos. Most of the hospital's income came from paying visitors so it was important to put on a good show. It took another century and more – until the late eighteenth and early nineteenth centuries in fact – before more enlightened hospital governors decided to stop all visits of this kind. It's a sad commentary on earlier attitudes to social class and mental illness that the mentally ill ceased to be whipped daily only when George III (1738–1820) became mad and his plight aroused widespread sympathy.

By the early 1810s it was time for the hospital to move once again. Plans had been drawn up for a new hospital on marshland south of the river. The land was cheap and it was even thought that the air, being cleaner, might do the patients some good.

The domed classical building we see today was designed by James Lewis (1750–1820) and finished in 1815. Patients were brought across London from Moorfields in a long sad line of Hackney cabs and under careful guard. And here the patients stayed until 1930 when a new hospital was built at Addington in Surrey. In 1936, having dithered about the fate of the old buildings, it was decided that rather than demolish them they should be used to provide an excellent home for the Imperial War Museum.

THE CURSE OF CENTRE POINT

1417

A curious tale surrounds the land on which the tall tower of Centre Point now stands. This busy area where Tottenham Court Road meets Oxford Street was once part of the area known as Seven Dials, centred on the church of St Giles that still stands a little behind Charing Cross Road. Until the mid-nineteenth century St Giles and Seven Dials was a dense warren of tiny courtyards and alleys where vast numbers of criminals and prostitutes lived and the police dared not go. Tucked away between Covent Garden to the south and Bloomsbury to the north the area is a strange survivor – it miraculously escaped wholesale redevelopment in the 1960s, for example.

A medieval leper hospital existed here amid open fields and well away from the City of London until the first developers came in the seventeenth century. They put up houses for artisans and skilled tradesmen, but within a few decades an area that had seemed a model development to Pepys when he visited it, had degenerated into a dark, overcrowded and fearsome place.

The old road to Oxford (now Oxford Street) runs along what is now the northern extremity of the district. It passes close by the parish church of St Giles, patron saint of lepers. For centuries church officials paid for a last drink at the Resurrection Gate for the condemned who passed the church and pub as they took their journey by cart from Newgate Prison in the east to the gallows at Tyburn (now Marble Arch) in the west.

The Resurrection Gate (rebuilt in the nineteenth century and renamed the Angel Inn) is still next to St Giles's Church and you can follow the route of the old Oxford Road as it winds its way through what were once fields.

St Giles's Church was completed in 1712 after the earlier church began to collapse. The walls of the old church, built in the twelfth century, had been gradually undermined by the huge number of burials. St Giles is one of a relatively small number of London churches that escaped Victorian 'improvements' and bombing in the Second World War.

The great seventeenth-century poet Andrew Marvel (1621–1678) is buried here and the pulpit from which John Wesley (1703–1791), the founder of Methodism, preached can still be seen. The plague of 1665, probably the worst outbreak in the whole history of that terrible disease, began here in St Giles. Here, too, lived London's ballad sellers, including James Catnach from whom we get the phrase catchpenny – meaning designed merely to sell quickly. The area was also famous for doctors and astrologers, trinket makers, bird sellers and pawnbrokers.

By the eighteenth century, when William Hogarth (1697–1764) depicted the area in his famous engraving 'Gin Lane', Seven Dials was a place avoided by anyone with the least pretensions to respectability. It was also pretty much beyond the reach of the authorities. Gin shops were everywhere and poverty and desperation made the inhabitants widely feared. If a criminal from the area was being taken from Newgate to Tyburn extra soldiers were drafted in to guard him because, as likely as not, his friends would mount a rescue operation as he stopped for his last drink at the Resurrection Gate and once he'd been carried off into the Rookeries, as Seven Dials was then known, he would never be found. Even with the presence of armed guards pitched battles still sometimes ensued and numerous condemned men escaped.

The name Seven Dials comes from the place, in the southern part of the district, where seven small streets meet to form a star. The plan is that of Sir Thomas Neale and dates back to 1694. There is still a small market here every weekday – the market has been here for more than a century – and many of the houses in the surrounding streets are basically eighteenth century, though much altered. Charles Dickens (1812–1870) called the area Tom All Alone's in *Bleak House* and something of the atmosphere Dickens must have known still lingers.

The obelisk at the centre of the star where the seven streets meet is a modern replacement, but from here narrow streets from the eighteenth century and one or two earlier houses radiate towards Covent Garden, Charing Cross Road, Shaftesbury Avenue and Long Acre.

Much of the original Rookeries, certainly that area north of St Giles's church, was destroyed in the 1880s to make way for Shaftesbury Avenue and New Oxford Street.

St Giles's Church once faced open fields but now faces into a narrow alleyway, so it's difficult to appreciate what a splendid sight it would have been when first built, as it gazed out across open ground towards Tottenham Lane, but the inside of the church is one of the chief glories of the whole area. For some extraordinary reason it is hardly ever visited either by local people or tourists. It is a quiet, forgotten backwater and therefore the perfect place to stop for a few moments to enjoy that rare thing – a London interior pretty much unchanged in almost 300 years.

But the strangest thing about this area is that businesses very rarely thrive – the shops and other outlets towards the top of Charing Cross Road, particularly around Centre Point, have constantly changed and the rate at which they tend to fail is far higher than the failure rate of comparable businesses elsewhere. Even Centre Point itself was a London scandal for a decade after it was built because it was so ugly that no one wanted to lease office space in it.

Why should the area be so unlucky? Rationalists would dismiss the idea but we know that in 1417 Sir John Oldcastle – the model for Shakespeare's Falstaff – was burned here for heresy on the orders of King Henry V. As the flames rose around him Sir John is said to have cursed the land and surrounding area on which he was burned as well as the executioner, the king and all his descendants. Perhaps the Curse of Falstaff still lingers.

GROPECUNT LANE

1450

We tend to think of the modern world as a place where anything goes – we take a very liberal view of swearing and sexual morality and we imagine that all other ages before ours were characterised by strict prudish morality, a morality typified by the Victorians who are popularly supposed to have covered the legs of their tables as the very idea of any sort of leg on display was shocking to them.

The Victorians may well have been excessively prudish, worthy and hypocritical, but it is completely wrong to imagine that all other earlier epochs were similar – there have been many periods in the past that have taken a far more liberal view of life in general than the modern age.

During Charles II's reign, for example, Nell Gwynn (1651–1687) was adored by Londoners who loathed the king's French wife and this despite the fact that Nell was always referred to as the king's whore. Whore in the seventeenth century seems to have lacked at least some of the harsher overtones that it now has.

Charles II himself cared little for traditional morality – he allowed plays to be written and performed that made the pursuit of pleasure, particularly sexual pleasure, the centre and mainspring of life. Puritan London was scandalised but there was little the religious could do as the plays had the king's sanction.

In medieval London too, sex was far more acceptable in a public context than it is now – anyone who looks at a map of London produced before 1450 will see several street names that are so extraordinary by our standards that they simply would not be allowed today.

Addle Street appears on these earlier maps, for example, and to a medieval Londoner Addle Street mean 'filthy spot'. Or take Fetter Lane, which still exists – in 1450 it meant the street of the dirty beggars.

Other names were dropped after the Reformation as the influence of killjoy Protestants came to dominate public life. Public holidays on saint's days were largely abandoned and many London street names were changed. Shiteburn Lane near Canon Street – so named because of the number of cess pits to be found here – was changed to the far more genteel sounding Sherborne Lane, a name it retains to this day.

But the most extraordinary street of all, that vanished with the arrival of the Reformation and the serious sensibility that seems to have accompanied it, was a small lane that ran north from Cheapside. It was called Gropecunt Lane for the simple reason that it was a famous haunt of prostitutes.

WHY WE SAY SIXES AND SEVENS

1490

Only London would retain something as dotty as a company of tailors who have had absolutely nothing to do with making clothes for more than three hundred years.

But like most London guilds, the Merchant Taylors have long since lost all connection with their original calling. Most guilds exist – again like the tailors – merely to administer ancient and sometimes more recent charitable bequests.

The Merchant Taylors – now rather sadly run by grey men in suits – still has some three hundred members and they administer a number of charities including alms houses in south London, a school in north London and a number of churches. But they have enjoyed – or suffered – a turbulent and fascinating history. Perhaps most interestingly, the Merchant Taylors are also responsible for that curious phrase where one describes a state of chaos or indecision as 'being at sixes and sevens'.

To find out how this odd phrase came into the language we need to take a brief look at the early history of the guild.

The Merchant Taylors, who were later joined by the Linen Armourers, originally made clothes – but most particularly a medieval jacket called a gambeson. This was a thick padded jacket – padded because it was worn in battle either under armour, by the nobility, or on its own by the common soldiers. As the gambeson fell out of use with the introduction of firearms and abandonment of swords and pikes, the Merchant Taylors moved on to make tents for the army until sometime in the seventeenth century even this became a pointless exercise.

The company received its charter as early as 1327 and is, as a result, considered one of the twelve great livery companies. These tend to be the most ancient companies and they include the mercers, drapers, fishmongers and goldsmiths. They were livery companies because members of particular guilds wore distinctive clothes (or livery).

In its Royal Charter of 1503, the guild is given its full name – 'The Gild of Merchant Taylors of the Fraternity of St. John Baptist in the City of London.'

Early in their history the guilds were jealous of their status and fought for their place in the order of precedence during any progress of the Lord Mayor across London.

After endless arguments with the Guild of Skinners about who should take sixth place in the order of precedence and who seventh, the Lord Mayor of London issued an order in the late fifteenth century to the effect that the Skinners and Merchant Taylors would alternate in precedence: in odd-numbered years the Merchant Taylors would be sixth in order; in even years the Skinners would take the sixth place and the Merchant Taylors would be seventh. Hence the phrase – to be at sixes and sevens.

The alternating precedence continues to this day.

THE HOUSE THAT SHAKESPEARE KNEW

1501

Few domestic houses in central London can lay claim to as many strange tales as a tall narrow house that stands on the south bank of the Thames looking towards St Paul's Cathedral.

The fact that the house is still standing is a remarkable tale in itself for this elegant narrow building – once part of a terrace – is the last remaining of the many Bankside houses that once lined the river here where Shakespeare's plays were first performed.

The house is still privately owned but when Henry VIII's future wife Catherine arrived from Spain in 1501 she stayed here and two centuries later when Christopher Wren (1632–1723) was building St Paul's he too stayed in the house to supervise the work on his great cathedral directly across the water.

Although it has been altered again and again over the years, the house nevertheless is basically sixteenth century. It stands almost next door to the re-created Globe Theatre and running down one side – sadly now closed to the public – is one of London's narrowest thoroughfares – Cardinal Cap Alley.

For the first few centuries after the house was built this was a poor and dangerous area – apart from the theatres (banished to the south side of the river by the more religious-minded members of the government who thought plays immoral) the area was also famous for its bear-baiting and cock-fighting pits, as well as for the sheer number of its brothels. The murder rate here was probably twice that of the city across the water and there are vague references to respectable citizens simply disappearing in the vicinity of Cardinals Wharf – at least one twentieth-century owner of the house said he would never excavate below the house for fear of what he might find!

ROBBING PETER TO PAY PAUL

1540

Few people today realise that Westminster Abbey is not the name of the great abbey church that stands at Westminster. The official name of the abbey is the Collegiate Church of St Peter at Westminster and it is from this name that the phrase robbing Peter to pay Paul comes. Today the phrase simply means taking money from, as it were, the left hand and giving it to the right or to pay one person at the pointless expense of another person.

The origins of the phrase lie in those decades after the Reformation of the mid-1500s that ended Britain's thousand-year monastic tradition. After Henry VIII's death his son Edward VI (1537–53) continued the work of giving monastic lands and money to his favourites. The new parish churches also competed for endowments and Westminster Abbey (St Peter's) petitioned the king endlessly for funding. So much so that he decided to punish the abbey by taking away the revenues St Peter's had long enjoyed from the Manor of Paddington and giving them to St Paul's, which had always been known as London's cathedral. Thus the Royal church lost out to the London cathedral – and the phrase robbing Peter to pay Paul came into the language.

VANISHED DUNGEONS REAPPEAR

1555

Many villages and country towns in England still have their ancient lock-ups – these are small, usually single-roomed buildings, often near the market square or by the side of a back street, that were once used to house those arrested before they could be taken to court and dealt with by local magistrates. They were also used simply to get someone unruly off the streets for the night – a drunk perhaps – and having sobered up the miscreant would then be released the next day.

The City of London had similar though usually larger lock-ups until fairly recent times – but in the City they were and are called compters. The original compter buildings have, like so much of London's history, been swept away but here and there the underground cells of former compters do survive.

Casual passers-by would be astonished to discover that what may well have once been the dungeons of the formerly infamous Wood Street Compter – situated in Mitre Court in the City – can still be seen complete with their chains and fetters. Mitre Court gets its name from the celebrated Mitre Tavern that once stood here – it is mentioned by countless writers and features in Ben Jonson's (1572–1637) play *Bartholomew Fair*.

The compter once housed some seventy prisoners. It was built in 1555 and was under the control of the sheriffs of London. It seems to have been used as a lock-up but also, curiously, as a debtor's prison and even to house the overflow of prisoners when nearby Newgate was full.

For centuries all trace of it was assumed to have vanished but early in the twentieth century the former dungeons were rediscovered. One wonders how many other parts of ancient London buildings remain underground and awaiting rediscovery.

The compter was unusual in reflecting precisely the social conditions outside the prison: it had three sections – the best section, the master's side as it was known, was for the wealthy and aristocratic; the knight's side was for those of some means, however small; and the hole was for the common people. The surviving cellars – now part of a nearby wine merchant – may well have been part of the hole, the most feared part of the prison and in which incarceration meant you were very likely to die from typhoid, cholera or some other waterborne disease.

THE QUEEN'S BOSOM ON SHOW

1597

Detailed descriptions of the London scene before 1600 are relatively rare. Those that exist only occasionally satisfy the modern desire for detail – published descriptions mention noble buildings, grand thoroughfares and monumental edifices, but they rarely describe what it was actually like to walk along the Strand, through the mud and the puddles, when the City wall still existed and the Strand was effectively a suburb where the rich had their riverside palaces.

But if physical, detailed descriptions are lacking we are lucky enough to have a number of wonderful descriptions of meetings with the great and the good.

When the French ambassador Andre Hurhault-Sieur de Maisse met Queen Elizabeth I for the first time in 1597 she had been on the throne for almost forty years, a remarkably long reign in an age of regular outbreaks of the plague and general medical ignorance.

It had taken more than a year for the French ambassador to finally fix a date for the meeting and his sense that this was a momentous and long-awaited event comes through in the detailed report he wrote afterwards.

De Maisse was led along a dark corridor to the audience chamber where the Queen sat alone on a low chair. Others in the room gathered in small groups at some distance from her. The ambassador made a low bow at the door and the Queen rose and came over to him. De Maisse takes up the story:

I kissed the fringe of her robe and she embraced me with both arms. She smiled at me, and began to apologise for not receiving me sooner. She said that the day before she had been very ill.

She was dressed in silver cloth, her dress with slashed sleeves lined with red taffeta. On her head she wore a garland and beneath it a great reddish-coloured wig, with a great number of spangles of gold and silver, and hanging down over her forehead some pearls, but of no great worth.

By this time the Queen was in her sixties. Her cheeks were sunken and her teeth were yellow and broken with many missing from her habit of continually eating sweets – in fact so many teeth were missing that it was difficult at times for De Maisse to understand what she was saying.

De Maisse noticed all this and was therefore doubly astonished to discover that she was actually half naked! He explains with evident astonishment that the Queen's dress was completely open down the front and that her breasts – which she continually handled and moved about – were completely open to view.

He says: 'Her bosom is somewhat wrinkled as well as one can see for the collar that she wears round her neck, but lower down her flesh is exceeding white and delicate, so far as one could see.'

The only explanation one can find at this distance in time is that the Queen, who could never be criticised or contradicted, really believed the stories her poets and painters told her – that she was the eternally youthful Virgin Queen. The creature she read about in the verses presented to her was daily confirmed by her courtiers' behaviour and she clearly believed it all – either that or by this time she was simply losing her marbles!

Queen Elizabeth I, who could never be criticised or contradicted, really believed the stories her poets and painters told her – that she was the eternally youthful Virgin Queen.

DERRICK'S DEATH CRANE

1610

All over the world wherever ships are unloaded the word derrick simply means a special type of crane that allows objects to be lifted and lowered but also swung horizontally. Few realise that the word and the design of the crane have their origins in one of London's most feared historical figures – a man whose name became a byword for death.

From 1388 until 1783 Londoners who were condemned to death were taken from Newgate Prison in the city in a tumbril – a primitive cart – that rolled through Holborn and on to the old Oxford Road (now Oxford Street) until it reached the western end of that road where today Oxford Street meets the Edgware Road. This place was then known as Tyburn. Throughout this long period Tyburn was chosen as the place of public execution precisely because it was open country. The authorities believed that public hangings acted as a deterrent to the rest of the population so when the hanging days came they wanted the crowds of spectators to be easily accommodated. Tyburn was perfect in this respect and 'Tyburn tree' became a euphemism for the gallows. Until the early seventeenth century the condemned stood in the back of the cart that had brought them to Tyburn until the hangman had the noose round their necks. The cart was then driven away and the victim was left dangling in midair. Death at this time was caused by slow strangulation – it wasn't until the nineteenth century and the introduction of the long drop that death by hanging became more or less instantaneous. The long drop meant that the neck was broken by the force of the victim's own weight rather than the slowly tightening effects of the noose as at Tyburn.

Gruesome stories from Tyburn are legion – relatives of the condemned would often run under the gallows, for example, and hang from the dangling man's legs to make sure he died quickly – but there was one major problem and it took the hangman Thomas Derrick to solve it. The problem was that on hanging days – which were always public holidays – there were usually too many to be hanged easily one at a time. Derrick introduced a gallows that could take up to a dozen or more at a time – the general shape of the new gallows took its inventor's name and, its shape being uncannily like that of the modern derrick crane, the name stuck.

Early references to hanging show how far into the consciousness of the London public the name derrick had penetrated. In 1608 an anonymous commentator wrote of a condemned highwayman: 'He rides his circuit with the Devil, and Derrick must be his host, and Tiburne the inne at which he will lighte. At the gallows, where I leave them, as to the haven at which they must all cast anchor, if Derrick's cables do but hold.'

JOHN DONNE, UNDONE

1631

The author of some of the greatest short poems of the seventeenth century, John Donne (1573–1631), is buried in St Paul's Cathedral where he was dean for a number of years. Donne is the author of many famous lines that have passed into the language – 'no man is an island', for example, and 'ask not for whom the bell tolls; it tolls for thee' – but in addition to writing verse he was a busy public man who sat as an MP in Elizabeth I's last parliament and worked for some time as a lawyer before taking holy orders.

By the time he entered the church he was already in middle age and probably a little embarrassed about his earlier versifying days. His piety certainly seems to have increased and towards the end of his life he commissioned his own monument, a life-size marble statue showing the poet in his shroud and peeping gloomily out from the folds of its hood. He posed for the sculptor in the very shroud that was later used to bury him.

Donne kept the monument itself in his house in the years up to his death and it was said that he sat in front of it every day when he said his prayers. When he died in 1631 it was placed in old St Paul's.

Nearly half a century later, of course, St Paul's burned down destroying pretty much everything within the church with one exception – John Donne's monument. Visitors today can still see the smoke-blackened lower parts of the marble – the only visible evidence of the Great Fire that consumed so much of London in 1666 –

but Donne peeps out from his hood unperturbed and even at the last his wit did not desert him. He wrote his own epitaph and the words are still there on the effigy: 'John Donne, Undone.'

A CHURCH THE WRONG WAY ROUND

1631

St Paul's Covent Garden is one of London's quirkiest churches. It was built as part of London's first planned square in 1631. Its architect – he was also the architect of the square and all the houses in it – was the great Inigo Jones, who had studied the work of Palladio in Italy and longed to produce something similar in London.

The idea of a square surrounded on three sides by collonaded walks was met with derision by Londoners but the Duke of Bedford, one of London's richest men and a great enthusiast for all things Italian, pressed ahead anyway.

The houses were built and were immediately popular with London's fashionable elite despite those early misgivings. But the church that Jones was asked to build at the west end of the square is bizarre because it is built the wrong way round.

Problems began when the Duke of Bedford, who seems to have been keen for the houses to be beautifully built, told Jones that he really didn't care much for the idea of a church at all and that therefore it was to be built as cheaply as possible – 'I want it little better than a barn,' he is reputed to have said – but Jones, being proud of his work, decided that he would build magnificently anyway: 'I will build the handsomest barn in England,' he claimed.

The planned design involved having a main entrance into the square – in other words at the east end of the church – but when Archbishop Laud got wind of the plan he was furious and, despite the fact that the church was almost complete, he ordered that the east end of the church be blocked up and that the entrance should be rebuilt at the west end where it remains to this day. The heavy portico at the east end, reminds us that this should originally have been the grand entrance.

It is ironic that the building on which least care was lavished, officially at least, is the only one to survive from Inigo Jones's time. During the years of Covent Garden's fame – which lasted until the end of the seventeenth century – the houses were proudly kept but as the fashionable moved out in the eighteenth century the square became famous for its brothels and gin shops.

This was caused partly by the growth of the vegetable market, which had started in the middle decades of the seventeenth century but had grown enormously a century later. With late-night revellers from the theatres, gin palaces and coffee houses open all night to service the market porters, the area lost its reputation as a genteel district and became the debauched squalid place depicted in Hogarth's 'Morning' from the series *Four Times of the Day*.

Inigo Jones's plan for a piazza made the word fashionable for decades and hundreds of London girls were christened 'Piazza' in the years up to 1650.

POET BURIED STANDING UP

1637

Westminster Abbey has long been the last resting place of the great, the good, the brave – and the poetically inclined. Among the more interesting epitaphs is T.S. Eliot's (1888–1965) splendidly enigmatic:

The communication of the dead
Is tongued with fire beyond the language of the living.

The lines come from Eliot's own great poem *Four Quartets*.

But the strangest monument in the abbey seems remarkably unassuming on the face of it – a small stone, moved from the floor of the abbey to a wall in the last century to protect it from wear and tear, reads simply: 'O rare Johnson'. The lines (including the mis-spelled surname – it should be Jonson!) were written by the now forgotten poet Jack Young and they refer to the great Elizabethan and Jacobean playwright Ben Jonson (1572–1637), who is buried in the abbey in a most unusual way.

Jonson, the son of a bricklayer, was extraordinarily lucky as a child to come to the attention of the antiquary William Camden, then a master at Westminster School. Camden paid for Jonson's schooling and in robbing us of a master bricklayer he gave us instead a master playwright.

Jonson's comic masterpieces *Every Man in his Humour*, *Bartholomew Fair*, *Volpone* and *The Alchemist* are unlikely ever to be forgotten and they were hugely popular in his lifetime, but despite his success Jonson was not a good businessman like his contemporary William Shakespeare.

Where Shakespeare invested his money in land and property, Jonson seems to have spent his on wild living – in a drunken brawl he killed a fellow poet and only escaped hanging because he was able to plead benefit of clergy. In Elizabethan England, bizarrely, a man who had committed murder but could read Latin was not executed. Instead his thumb would be branded – as was Jonson's – with the letter M.

Towards the end of his life and still living in poverty Jonson is supposed to have discussed his funeral arrangements with the Dean of Westminster. 'I am too poor to be buried in the abbey,' he is reported to have said, 'And no one will lay out my funeral charges. Six feet long by two feet wide is too much for me. Two feet by two feet will do.'

The dean is said to have immediately promised Jonson he could have his tiny area in what was to become known as Poets' Corner, clearly thinking that Jonson intended only to have a small memorial attached to the spot. In fact Jonson was properly buried in the abbey when the time came – he did it by arranging to have himself buried standing bolt upright in his grave where he remains to this day. It was his final joke.

In the 1840s work on the floor of the abbey disturbed the grave and Jonson's leg bones were found standing upright; his skull was intact too and apparently still with red hair attached to it!

Other graves in Westminster Abbey have strange stories attached to them – the poet Byron (1788–1824) was not commemorated here until 1967 because of his disreputable lifestyle (despite the fame of his poetry) and even Shakespeare had to wait until 1740 for a monument to be erected for him. The difficulty for the authorities when they thought of Shakespeare was reconciling themselves to the fact that despite being a commoner with only a relatively rudimentary education he became and remains the greatest writer in the English language – perhaps in any language. The same feeling of unease has fuelled numerous claims over the centuries that other more aristocratic scribblers are responsible for the plays and poems and merely used Shakespeare's name.

A SQUARE OF WONDERS

1641

There are lots of wonderfully odd things about Lincoln's Inn Fields. The name reminds us that this was for centuries open ground where the lawyers from the Inns of Court enjoyed walking, so much that when building began in the 1640s a deputation from the lawyers to the builders persuaded them not to cover the whole site with new houses but instead to leave the central area open, which is just as it remains to this day.

Other oddities about the square include Sir John Soane's (1753–1837) extraordinary house – rarely can a single relatively small house have been so stuffed with antiquities. Special cupboards and sliding display cases of great ingenuity and complexity had to be built at great expense to house Sir John's vast collection in such a small space. The house is now open to the public.

The square was and is also home to the Royal College of Surgeons – in earlier times tumbrils travelled regularly across the square carrying the bodies of the recently executed for dissection at the college. And in the college museum is the skeleton of Jonathan Wilde, the famous highwayman who was also the model for John Gay's (1685–1732) celebrated character Macheath in *The Beggar's Opera*.

The square was the scene of an encounter that typified the reasons for the seventeenth-century Londoner's love of 'pretty, witty' Nell Gwynn, Charles II's favourite mistress. Stories about Nell abound but two of the best concern her time here in Lincoln's Inn Fields. Travelling here from

Covent Garden one summer day she found herself surrounded by a mob that jostled her coach. She quickly realised that the angry crowd thought she was Charles's very unpopular French mistress, Catholic Louise de Keroualle (1649–1734). With great presence of mind Nell straightaway stuck her head out the window and shouted: 'Pray good people be civil, I am the Protestant whore!'

On another occasion she sat in her house in Lincoln's Inn – number 58 – with her son by Charles II playing nearby. The boy was aged about five. Nell was irritated that Charles had so far done nothing for the boy but she knew that direct appeals to him would do nothing. When he arrived to see her he played with his son for a while but the boy then ran off to the other side of the room and wouldn't return. Nelly saw her chance: 'Come here, you little bastard!' she shouted. Charles was horrified. 'Why do you use that terrible name?' he asked. 'Well, you have given him no other,' she replied. Charles promptly made the boy Duke of St Albans with land and an income that his descendants enjoy to this day.

But without question the oddest aspect of Lincoln's Inn Fields is that its dimensions are precisely those of the base of the Great Pyramid at Giza!

WHERE TO GET YOUR COAT OF ARMS

1666

The British are obsessed with social class – it's a truism but one that reverberates through history. In earlier times the rising middle classes tried desperately to find an ancestor or two who would introduce a hint of blue blood to the family. Thomas Hardy's *Tess of the D'Urbervilles* reveals that even a poor country girl could be fooled into thinking that her ancestors were aristocrats and that somehow this meant her whole life should change. Then there was Shakespeare, who made every effort to persuade the College of Arms to accept his family's entitlement to a banner that would proclaim them gentlemen through and through. He failed but the institution to which he applied for his coat of arms still exists in the heart of London.

The vast mystery of family coats of arms, their history, design, conception and meaning, can be traced to an ancient, crooked, but still magnificent building in Queen Victoria Street in the heart of the old City and close to the river.

A miraculous survivor of German bombs, the seventeenth-century College of Arms is home to a bizarre range of officials who can be grouped into the royal heralds and the kings at arms. There are three kings at arms – Garter, Norroy and Clarenceux. The royal heralds are York, Lancaster, Windsor, Chester, Somerset and Richmond. The college also houses the pursuivants – Rouge Dragon, Blue Mantle,

Rouge Croix and Portcullis. Each of these titles is given to one man. Bizarrely, the head of the college – the Earl Marshall – is always the Duke of Norfolk. Norfolk is England's premier dukedom but the family has always traditionally been Catholic and at least one had his head lopped off for treachery.

The role, complexity and purpose of the various jobs carried out at the College of Arms would take a whole book to explain but suffice it to say that even today, more than five centuries after the college was established, no one, whether company or individual, is allowed to design and use a coat of arms without the permission of the college and there are strict rules about what exactly can appear on a coat of arms. There are a number of cases where those who broke the rules have been fined heavily for so doing.

Most of the terms used by the college are based on a curious medieval mix of Norman French (still current in elevated circles for a century and more after the Norman invasion), Latin and Middle English.

The College of Arms still has the charters and other documentation that survived the Great Fire of 1666 when the fifteenth-century building on the same site was burned down. All the paperwork was bundled into a boat and taken across the river.

Traditionally – though this is apparently not the case now – jobs in the college were given to important friends of important people, which may explain the long line of eccentrics, drunks and lunatics who have snoozed away the decades in the ancient panelled rooms of this delightful building.

Among the most eccentric was William Oldys (1696–1761), apparently given a job as herald because the Duke of Norfolk had enjoyed reading Oldys's book about Sir Walter Raleigh. Dukes of Norfolk, remember, always get the job of Earl Marshall, whose main role is to organise state occasions – funerals, weddings and coronations. Oldys spent his days and evenings in a local pub but employed a man to carry him back – completely drunk – to the college before midnight. If he was later than that it meant a fine. Oldys is best remembered today for a strange little poem he wrote towards the end of his life:

Busy curious thirsty fly
Drink with me and drink as I.
Freely welcome to my cup
Couldst thou sip and sip it up.
Make the most of life you may
Life is short and wears away.

THE ULTIMATE CELEBRITY STREET

1675

One of the most interesting thoroughfares in London is Buckingham Street – a short street of late seventeenth- and early eighteenth-century houses that runs up from the Embankment towards the Strand and a little to the east of Charing Cross Station.

The houses are modest and one or two have been rebuilt but this short street can lay claim to having housed more celebrities than any other comparable street in London.

When London's first great speculative builder – the first modern developer – Nicholas Barbon (1640–1698) bought the land at the end of the seventeenth century he immediately began building the sort of houses that would appeal to the fashionable. Most were complete by 1675.

Number 10 Buckingham Street was once the home of David Hume (1711–1776), the brilliant Scottish philosopher and father of the Enlightenment. Later on the house was lived in by the famous postimpressionist painter Henri Rousseau (1844–1910). Diarist Samuel Pepys (1633–1703) lived both at number 12 and at number 14. Number 12 was later occupied by Queen Anne's Lord Treasurer Robert Harley (1661–1724), who invited Jonathan Swift (1644–1718) and William Penn (1667–1745) (of Pennsylvania fame) to dine with him. Two painters lived in the house at different times – William Etty (1787–1849) and Clarkson Stanfield (1793–1867). The scientist Humphrey Davy (1778–1829) carried out some of his most important experiments in the cellar! Peg Woffington (1720–1760), a celebrated beauty and one of the greatest eighteenth-century actresses, lived at number 9. The Russian Peter the Great (1672–1725) stayed for a while at number 15, while Henry Fielding (1707–1754), the creator of *Tom Jones*, lived here too, as did – a century later – Charles Dickens (1812–1870). Samuel Taylor Coleridge (1772–1834) lived at number 21. Most bizarrely of all, Napoleon Bonaparte (1769–1821) stayed in a house in the street – exactly which one is disputed – for a short period during 1791.

A MOUSETRAP ON THE HEAD

1690

Until the 1980s there was still a strange little jewellery shop tucked away in a corner of one of the ancient Inns of Court. The shop, known as the Silver Mousetrap, had traded continually from these premises since 1690, but if the survival of a shop that long in London is remarkable then the origin of the shop's name is even more noteworthy.

The name dates back to a time when rich fashionable women would spend a day or two having their hair turned into an extraordinary sculpture. First the hair would be piled as high as possible – perhaps with the addition of artificial hair – and then plaster birds might be added to make it look as if birds were nesting in the hair and perhaps a small carved ship or a tree or simply a mass of artificial flowers. Occasionally a mix of all these things and more would be built into the structure of the hair, which was stiffened with flour, chalk dust or arsenic powder.

The problem with these fabulous creations is that they took so long to make that they had to be slept in for weeks at a time and until the style was changed the hair could not be washed. This led to a serious problem with mice.

Today, when we have a range of sophisticated chemicals to control mice and other pests, it is difficult to imagine what it was like when there were no really effective ways to control mice, rats, bedbugs and fleas – beds were routinely infested with bugs until the twentieth century and houses collapsed when wood-boring insects had done their work for long enough; walls and ceiling voids were commonly filled with mice which people tended to ignore, since the business of trying to remove or kill them was simply impossible. Even if it had been possible to eliminate a particular infestation newcomers would soon move in to take their place.

When a woman of fashion slept with her enormous head of firmly fixed hair mice invariably found their way into it, and even for a population that had learned to put up with the presence of various rodents this was too much.

For a woman embarrassed at the prospect of a mouse popping out of her hair during lunch or supper there was only one solution. A trip to The Silver Mousetrap, where elegant ladylike mousetraps made in silver were available. Having bought two or three of these things the woman of fashion, on retiring for the night, would place them strategically around her head. If the mice came out while she slept they would with any luck be caught in one or other of the traps. Users were warned not to roll about too much in their sleep lest an unwary nose or ear set off one of the traps!

WHEN PRISON MARRIAGES WERE ALL THE RAGE

1696

It is hard to believe now but 15 per cent of all marriages conducted in Britain during most of the late seventeenth and early eighteenth centuries were actually conducted in London's Fleet Prison, or more precisely in what were known as the Rules of the Fleet – an area bounded roughly by Fleet Lane, the Old Bailey, Farringdon Street and Ludgate Hill.

Today almost none of the maze of alleys and courtyards that once existed here survive. But in the eighteenth century the mass of cheap lodging houses within the Rules of the Fleet provided homes for Fleet prisoners who'd been given special privileges.

The Fleet was a debtors' prison but, under the strange rules that dated back to medieval times, debtors who provided suitable security were let out of the prison itself on the understanding that they would not leave the Rules of the Fleet. Here they could live and carry on their jobs and professions until such time as their debts had been paid and they were released. But within the Rules imprisoned clergymen (and there were a surprisingly large number of imprisoned clergymen) were permitted to conduct entirely legal marriages.

The first Fleet marriage of which records survive took place in 1613 but by the late seventeenth century an odd ecclesiastical law meant that there was an explosion in the number of marriages carried out in the Fleet.

In 1696 the law changed so that clergymen who married couples without first declaring the banns were prosecuted – as they were beneficed clergymen they might lose their livings. Clergymen in the Fleet were by definition unbeneficed (i.e. they had no parishes) and could not therefore be prosecuted as the law specifically referred to beneficed clergymen, so anyone who wanted to marry without their parents' permission could do so only at the Fleet.

Couples arrived in their hundreds and then thousands and there was little the authorities could do. Some have argued that the authorities deliberately left this loophole open to reduce the number of illicit relationships.

As well as within the prison itself, Fleet marriages took place in coffee houses, lodging rooms and shops of all kinds (from booksellers to bakers). What's more, it was possible to be married at any time of the day or night, seven days a week throughout the year – the Fleet in early eighteenth-century London had the sort of reputation for marriages that Las Vegas has today.

More than two hundred and fifty thousand couples are recorded as marrying in the Fleet before the rules changed and the prison was demolished – some of the marriages were no doubt forced or fraudulent but many couples' motives were entirely honourable. They were merely attracted by the speed and relative cheapness of a Fleet marriage.

PIG FAT AND FACE POWDER

1700

Among the dottiest people who ever lived in London was Lady Lewson, famed throughout the middle decades of the eighteenth century for her bizarre lifestyle.

Records suggest she was born in 1700 or perhaps 1701 in Essex Street just north of the Strand. Mrs Lewson – or Lady Lewson as she was afterwards known – married a rich elderly merchant when she was just nineteen and moved to his house at Clerkenwell, then a quiet village on the edge of London.

Her husband died when she was only twenty-six, but from that time until her death in about 1800, she hardly ever left the house. Every day she made sure all the beds in the house were made up, although no one ever came to stay. She was highly superstitious: in over sixty years she never cleaned a window in the house, fearing they would be broken in the process or that the person cleaning them might be injured. And she refused to allow anything to be moved in any room, believing that it might make her catch cold.

In summer she was sometimes seen reading in her garden in attire which would have been far more appropriate to the fashion of about 1690, with 'ruffs and cuffs and fardingales', and she always wore her hair powdered and piled high on her head over a stiff horsehair frame.

She believed washing was highly dangerous and would lead to some 'dreadful disorder'. Instead she smeared her face and neck with pig's fat, on top of which she applied a liberal quantity of pink powder.

When Lady Lewson died it was the talk of London – her house was opened up to mourners and the curious who found a time capsule unchanged in more than seventy years.

GOING TO KNIGHTSBRIDGE BY BOAT

1736

The Serpentine Lake in Hyde Park is one of London's best-known landmarks. It has an unusual history in that it was originally not a lake at all but a stretch of one of London's many small rivers, each a tributary of the Thames.

Just outside the western wall of the old City of London was the Fleet River, which ran down what is now Farringdon Street through Ludgate Circus and thence into the Thames. Further west, but again running north–south, the Tyburn flowed down what is now Edgware Road on through Victoria and parallel with Vauxhall Bridge Road before reaching the Thames.

The Westbourne flowed from Hampstead Heath down through west London and across Hyde Park, down modern Sloane Street and across Sloane Square before reaching the Thames just to the east of Christopher Wren's magnificent Chelsea Hospital.

It was Charlotte, George II's queen, who decided that Hyde Park needed a great lake. The park itself had been the property of the Crown since Henry VIII took it from the monks of Westminster in 1536 (the monks had in their turn no doubt taken it from someone else) to use as a hunting ground. The public at this time were strictly forbidden to enter the park.

Early in the seventeenth century James I allowed limited access to the park but only for the nobility and aristocracy. Charles I opened the park to the public in 1637 and created The Ring – the sandy road that allowed the fashionable for the next three centuries to parade and be seen on foot and on horseback and in their carriages.

Queen Charlotte decided the lake would make the park far more attractive so the River Westbourne was dammed and excavations began to produce the splendid stretch of water we see today.

But the first phase of the work left the River Westbourne flowing above ground as a way to control the level in the lake. In 1736 a massive flood led to the Westbourne bursting its banks and the whole of the area south of the Serpentine down through the Albert Gate, through Knightsbridge and Belgravia was under several feet of water for weeks. The Thames watermen made the most of an opportunity and rowed sightseers from Chelsea up to Knightsbridge and beyond. At this time most of the roads around London were impassable to wheeled vehicles for most of the year anyway so the sudden appearance of extra water for boat travel – always the preferred mode of transport for Londoners – made Hyde Park far more popular than it would otherwise have been.

AIR BATHING IN CRAVEN STREET

1757

It's a little-known fact that Benjamin Franklin (1706–1790), one of the four men who signed the American Declaration of Independence, lived for 16 years in a crooked little terraced house in Craven Street, a street that, before the building of the Embankment in the 1860s, ran down to the mud banks of the River Thames.

Craven Street survived the building of the Embankment – which effectively pushed the river back two hundred yards – as well as the building of Charing Cross Station, the German bombs of the Second World War and the obsession with redevelopment in the 1960s. Virtually all the houses in the street are eighteenth century although most have been over-restored to create office space.

No. 36, Franklin's old home, is one of the few to survive with its interior virtually intact – what we see today are the doors, chimneypieces and staircases once used by Franklin himself and it was here that Franklin pursued some of his more eccentric interests.

Franklin was a great friend of Erasmus Darwin (1731–1802), Matthew Boulton (1728–1809) and Josiah Wedgwood (1730–1795), all members of the Lunar Society, a Midlands-based dining club of industrialists and engineers who embraced every new invention of the late eighteenth century – the first great period of the Industrial Revolution.

Franklin was passionate about science long before he became passionate about American politics. He was also a noted eccentric and if you had wandered along Craven Street early in the eighteenth century on a summer's day you might easily have seen Franklin sitting in his downstairs drawing-room window completely naked!

He was a great believer in the medical benefits of what was then called 'Air bathing' – a form of recreation to which William Blake (1757–1827) was also partial in the garden of his house across the river in Lambeth.

Franklin was also fascinated by electricity, dentistry, chemistry and optics. Like his friends in the Birmingham factories he believed that science would lead to a better life for mankind. He was also keen on practical experiments. He was part of that group of inventors who organised public demonstrations of electricity by spinning a glass ball against a leather pad to produce a huge build-up of static. As one contemporary put it: 'Franklin is a lightning rod philosopher who goes to the Charterhouse School each week, catches a charity boy, strings him up on silk cords, rubs him with glass and extracts sparks from his nose.'

Franklin's other exploits included swimming in the Thames at Chelsea on his back while paring his nails. He did it just to prove it could be done and he also had a set of wooden false teeth made.

The great radical writer William Cobbett (1763–1835) disliked Franklin, describing him as 'That crafty and lecherous old hypocrite', but he was much loved by his Birmingham industrialist friends.

When his house in Craven Street was being restored in the 1990s a mass of human bones was found buried in the basement – at first the police suspected a serial killer but it turns out that Franklin lodged with William Hewson, a doctor who ran an anatomy school from the Craven Street house. The bones showed evidence of surgery – skulls had been trepanned, for example, and leg bones mended.

But whatever went on in this particular house we know there was a roaring trade in corpses in eighteenth-century London. The 'resurrection men', as those who stole bodies from graveyards were known, would have rowed to the river steps at the bottom of Craven Street before delivering their gruesome cargo – human bones from babies, teenagers, the middle aged and elderly were all found buried here. The other source of at least some of these bones would have been the gallows that then stood just behind the garden wall of No. 30.

While he lived at Craven Street, Franklin complained about the smoky fire in his rooms – the metal damper he invented to solve the problem still exists in the house.

Before the Embankment was built Craven Street ran down to the edge of the Thames and, like the Londoners of old, you can still take a boat from here to the Tower of London or to Greenwich. Famous residents included Henrich Heine (1797–1856), the German poet, and Grinling Gibbons (1648–1721), the great woodcarver. The author James Smith wrote a splendid satirical poem about the lawyers who were his neighbours in the street during the early nineteenth century:

In Craven Street Strand, ten attorneys find place
And ten dark coal barges are moored at its base.
Fly honesty Fly, seek some safer retreat
For there's craft in the river and craft in the street.

A poetical lawyer responded with the following verse:

Why should honesty fly to some safer retreat
From attorneys and barges god rot 'em
For the lawyers are just at the top of the street
And the barges are just at the bottom.

Benjamin Franklin's house – the scene of so many of these bizarre tales – is now open to the public having recently been beautifully restored.

HIGHLAND SOIL IN WESTMINSTER

1760

The British are notoriously eccentric and as a general rule it is probably pretty safe to say that the richer the individual the greater the eccentricity. One of the most eccentric London residents of all time has to be the eighteenth-century Earl of Fife. A staunch Jacobite who hated the repression of the Scots that followed their defeat at Culloden in 1745, he was determined to get the better of the English whenever he could.

But the Earl was in a tricky position – from 1760 on he found that he had to visit London regularly for business reasons and the easiest way to do this, then as now for the very rich, was to buy or build a house. But the Earl's motives were not entirely financial – he hated the idea of being in London at all and by building his own house he could avoid the horror of having to stay in an English hotel run by the hated English.

But even if he built his own house in London it would still be on English soil, which was anathema to the good Earl. His solution was to buy a plot of land on Horse Guards Avenue near Whitehall. He then arranged, at enormous expense, to have a merchant ship filled with Scottish soil and sailed down the coast and up the Thames to Whitehall Steps. From here the soil was carried up Whitehall in a series of carts and dumped on the Earl's new acre of ground. Once the detested English soil had been completely covered with far superior Scottish soil the Earl went ahead and built his new house.

Sadly not a trace of that house remains today; but since we have no evidence that the soil beneath the house was ever removed we must assume that the land here is still as Scottish as it was in 1760.

WHY ACTORS SAY 'BREAK A LEG!'

1766

The theatrical phrase 'break a leg!' – a good-luck wish before a performance – has its origins in a little-known but curiously endearing story from the Theatre Royal in the Haymarket.

When Samuel Foote (1720–1777) took over the running of the theatre in the second half of the eighteenth century he knew he was taking a risk because the theatre, then known as the Little Theatre, did not have a licence – theatre licences could only be granted by the King and the King resolutely refused to grant the Little Theatre a licence because a previous owner had published a number of pamphlets attacking the government and the Crown.

Foote was undaunted and attempted by every means to obtain the necessary royal warrant but all to no avail. He found a way round the problem temporarily by not charging those who came to see his plays. Audiences could get in free but Foote made up for what he failed to take at the door by charging hugely inflated prices for coffee and food during the intervals.

This infuriated the Crown and made it less likely that Foote would ever get the royal seal of approval, but a bizarre turn of events changed all that. The King's brother the Duke of York overheard Foote boasting about his horsemanship and challenged him to ride with him the following morning. Foote agreed but the Duke deliberately brought a horse that had never been ridden. Foot inevitably was thrown and badly injured – he broke a leg and spent weeks recovering. The Duke was stricken with remorse and to make up for what he had done he granted

Foote the royal licence for which he had waited so long. It was 1766 and the Little Theatre in the Haymarket became the Theatre Royal, a title it has enjoyed uninterrupted ever since. The phrase 'break a leg' passed into the language – a sign that present disaster can quickly be transformed into future success.

BYRON GETS BURNED

1768

Albemarle Street just off Piccadilly was for more than two centuries the home of one of the world's most extraordinary publishers: John Murray, who came to London in 1768 to seek his fortune.

Born in 1739 he was originally John McMurray but dropped the Mc on coming to London after a number of years' service as a lieutenant in the marines. Murray's first office was in Fleet Street where, quite by chance, he took over No. 32, the site of Wynkyn de Word's printing press established in 1500. But within a few years he had moved to 50 Albemarle Street from which office, among a host of dazzling writers, the firm published David Hume, Byron, Jane Austen, Charles Darwin, Gladstone and Sir Arthur Conan Doyle.

By 2005 – some two hundred and thirty years later – the firm was still being run from this small house at 50 Albemarle Street, making it the oldest independent book publisher in the world. The original fireplaces were still here until the company was finally sold in 2003; the alcoves and odd corners remain in what is still in essence an eighteenth-century house.

Little had changed in more than two centuries by the time the company was sold and, most astonishing of all, the firm was always run by a John Murray – the last was the seventh direct male descendant of the founder.

It was only when the seventh John Murray's two sons (neither incidentally called John) decided they did not want to go into the family business that the firm was reluctantly sold to a huge multinational whose name – for the sake of decency – had probably better not be mentioned.

There are moves to make 50 Albemarle Street into a museum but in the meantime the company's archives – thousands of letters and other documents relating to its history and the host of famous authors it published – are likely to be sold, at the time of writing, for as much as £40 million. Most of the material has never been catalogued or seen.

Everything to do with John Murray is remarkable but most intriguing of all was a meeting that took place in 1824 in an upstairs room in front of a fireplace that is still there. John Murray the second met with the executors of Byron's estate shortly after the poet's death. They held in their hands two manuscript volumes of the great poet's diaries but they were so scandalised by the contents that they decided to throw them on the fire and thus was lost for ever what would have been one of the greatest literary treasures of the Romantic age. Perhaps, too, the publisher was getting his revenge on the poet who would often arrive in the office and while talking to Murray would practise his fencing by lunging at the various books around the room and tearing holes in them with his sword!

OBSESSED BY SNUFF

1776

Today drug taking is frowned on by the respectable, but in earlier times there was no stigma at all attached to those who regularly took opium – famous drug-addict authors like Thomas de Quincey (whose *Confessions of an English Opium Eater* was published in 1821), poets such as Samuel Taylor Coleridge and members of the royal family were enthusiastic drug takers and they would have laughed at the idea that taking opium was somehow a bad thing. However, opium was always the drug of choice for the relatively well off – lower down the social scale, the most popular drug of all before cigarettes was snuff. Snuff taking was almost universal in Georgian and Victorian England, but few were as enthusiastic about powdered tobacco as the infamous Margaret Thomson.

When she made her will in the early part of the nineteenth century Mrs Thomson, who lived in Essex Street just off the Strand, stipulated that the beneficiaries of her will would not get a penny if they failed to ensure that her coffin was filled with all the snuff handkerchiefs that were unwashed at the time of her death; she also wanted to be surrounded with freshly ground snuff in her coffin. Six of the greatest snuff takers in the parish were requested to be her pallbearers, and each was asked to wear a snuff-coloured hat. Six girls were instructed to walk behind the hearse, each with a box of snuff which they were to take copiously for their refreshment as they went along.

The priest who officiated at the ceremony was invited to take as much snuff as he desired during the service, and Mrs Thomson left him five guineas on condition that he partook of snuff during and throughout the funeral proceedings. In return for a bequest of snuff, her servants were instructed to walk in front of the funeral procession throwing snuff on the ground and on to the crowd of onlookers. And throughout the long day of the funeral, snuff was to be distributed to all comers from the door of the deceased's house.

HOW THE BRISTOL HOTEL GOT ITS NAME

1778

London still has at least one Bristol Hotel – it is in Berkeley Street, W1 – but during the late eighteenth century the city boasted a profusion of hotels, all called Bristol. Outside London and indeed right across Europe the situation was the same. There were Bristol hotels wherever travellers tended to stop for the night.

The reason has to do with one of London's oddest characters – a man largely forgotten today but in his lifetime a byword for luxury and extravagance.

Born in 1730, Edward Hervey studied at Westminster and Cambridge. Through the influence of his brother, Lord Bristol, he was made Bishop of Cloyne, though as he himself admitted he had absolutely no connection with or interest in Ireland. However, he soon started manoeuvring for the bishopric of Derry, which was worth more money than Cloyne, again using the influence of his brother, and he was successful. When he heard the news he was playing leapfrog with his fellow clergy in the garden at Cloyne Palace and is reported to have shouted: 'I will jump no more, gentlemen. I have surpassed you all, and jumped from Cloyne to Derry!'

He was thirty-nine, married, and earning a reputation as an eccentric largely because he was sympathetic to the local Catholic population which, under English rule, could own virtually nothing nor hold any office of any worth. His outspokenness on the subject almost led to him being impeached for treason, and Walpole, Charles James Fox and most other English parliamentarians thought him mad, bad and dangerous to know.

He got nowhere with his radical views, however, and developed instead his personality. He built three huge houses, his favourite being the size of Blenheim Palace, perched on a cliff top at Lough Foyle. On the death of his brother in 1778 he became Lord Bristol and went to live in London.

His house parties – held in his huge London residence – were legendary; he would often invite the fattest clergy to stay and then, after dinner, make them race round the house against each other. If he invited the clergy wives he always sprinkled flour outside their bedroom doors to see if he could catch them moving about between bedrooms during the night.

In his latter years he rarely visited Ireland and spent most of his time getting drunk in London and travelling extensively in France and Italy, where he spent so lavishly that hotel owners vied with each other to make their hotels more attractive to the great man. Hundreds renamed their hotels after him in order to indicate to other potential customers that the great Lord Bristol had stayed there and dozens retain the name 'Bristol' to this day.

Towards the end of his life he received a 'round robin' criticising him for being absent for so long from his parish, but he sent each signatory an inflated pig's bladder containing a dried pea along with a copy of the following verse:

Three large bluebottles sat upon three bladders.
Blow bottle flies, blow; burst, blow bladder burst.
A new-blown bladder and three blue balls
Make a great rattle.
So rattle bladder rattle.

He died in 1803 aged seventy-three.

EIGHTEENTH-CENTURY VIAGRA

1779

Dr James Graham was a genuine doctor, but at a time when all genuine doctors were by modern standards complete frauds – the evidence for this can be seen in the fact that, for example an Edinburgh medical textbook of 1750 listed under 'valuable remedies' the following: horse dung, pig skulls, frogspawn, ants' eggs and ground-up human skulls.

But Dr Graham, though interested in medicine, was far more interested in money, which is why when he left his native Edinburgh for London in around 1774 he set up his surgery in the most fashionable part of town – St James.

By 1779 he had realised that an important medical affliction was not at that time being addressed by any medical practitioner. Dr Graham decided that he would corner the market in cures for infertility. He set up his Temple of Health in Pall Mall and took large expensive advertisements in the London newspapers. In these he made outlandish claims for the extraordinary benefits of what he called his 'Celestial Bed'. The idea was that infertile couples would seek out the doctor, ask his advice and then be directed to his own certain cure: the Celestial Bed. Not only would the bed cure infertility – it would also ensure that any children conceived on it were far stronger and more beautiful 'in mental as well as in bodily endowments than the present puny race of Christians'.

The bed could only be rented and couples paid exorbitant sums for the privilege – perhaps as much as £100 per session. Graham claimed that while an infertile couple had sex on his bed he would activate a mechanism that would surround the happy couple with 'celestial fire' and cherishing vapours. He would also pump through glass tubes the very same perfumes used by the Turkish Sultan to guarantee that he could keep up with the demands of his enormous harem.

Despite the bed's mattress being made from the baked tails of sexually rapacious 'English stallions', history does not record the levels of satisfaction enjoyed by Dr Graham's customers, but we do know that within a few years of the advertisements appearing the good doctor vanished from the London scene.

BEAU BRUMMEL'S BLUE NOSE

1794

Beau Brummel (1778–1840), close friend of the Prince Regent and arbiter of fashion in the early part of the nineteenth century, had in his younger days been an officer in the 10th Light Dragoons. When he wasn't soldiering he lived in some splendour in a house in Chesterfield Street in London's Mayfair, where he taught the Prince of Wales to tie his own cravat (the prince never quite mastered the art) and where endless numbers of the fashionable came to be passed fit to be seen in society by the great arbiter of taste.

Brummel had been commissioned into the dragoons by his friend the Prince Regent but despite his fashion sense he was a hopeless incompetent when it came to matters military, for Brummel was one of England's most forgetful soldiers.

His biggest difficulty was that he could never remember the faces of the men in the troop he commanded – it was a chronic problem that led to huge embarrassment and there seemed to be no solution but, then as now, incompetence was no bar to high rank in the British army provided one had the right accent and background, which of course Brummel had.

Then Brummel himself came up with a solution – he noticed that one of the men in his troop had a very blue nose and he ordered that this man should always be in the front rank when the men were assembled. If Brummel then failed to identify his troop of men he would need only to look for that blue nose to know that he was in the right place.

All went well until one day at the Horse Guards in Whitehall. Brummel sat immaculately dressed on his splendid horse and was approached by a senior officer who demanded what he thought he was doing.

Brummel stared in blank amazement at the squadron commander.

'You are with the wrong troop,' he was told in no uncertain terms.

Panic-stricken, Brummel stared around and with a sigh of relief spotted the blue nose in the men lined up just in front of him.

'I think, if I may say so, you are mistaken,' he replied. 'I'm not so foolish as to be unable to recognise my own troop.' But what Brummel, who famously spent most of his army career in front of a mirror, did not know was that there had been a troop reorganisation and 'blue nose' had been moved to another troop without his knowledge.

BETTING ON CATS

1795

Bond Street is unusual in that unlike almost every other London district it has never lost its reputation as a fashionable place to shop. It's also unusual in that it is the only street that runs right across Mayfair from Piccadilly to Oxford Street. Despite this, the street is actually two streets – the southern section, which runs as far north as Burlington Gardens, was built in the early 1680s by Sir Thomas Bond, the northern section in the 1720s.

Most of the original seventeenth- and eighteenth-century houses have now gone (Aspreys' shop is an exception) but from the first the street was so popular as a shopping destination that it also became an important place simply to be seen, so much so that it began to rival both the famous pleasure gardens at Ranelagh and Rotten Row.

Among those who regularly promenaded here in the late eighteenth century was the Prince of Wales, later the Prince Regent. The prince was a notorious gambler who would bet on almost anything – he once took a bet on which of two raindrops would be first to run to the bottom of a window – but he was also something of a simpleton who was regularly fleeced by his gambling-mad courtiers.

The politician Charles James Fox (1749–1806), a supporter of American independence, anti-slavery campaigner and Britain's first Foreign Secretary, once got the better of the Prince of Wales in a bizarre bet made while walking down Bond Street one sunny afternoon.

Fox noticed a cat lounging at the side of the street so he suggested to the Prince that each should choose one side of the street and then wager who would see the greatest number of cats during a walk from one end of the street to the other.

Fox was crafty enough to choose the side of the street in full sun rather than the shady side and at the end of their walk he had spotted thirteen cats to the Prince's grand total of none. The baffled prince was forced to hand over the entire contents of his purse.

THE MOLE THAT KILLED A KING

1806

St James's Square retains just a few of its original early eighteenth-century houses, but this small square has been home at various times to an extraordinary list of the famous and the infamous – Gladstone and Pitt lived here along with half a dozen earls, several dukes and numerous royal mistresses. In fact within a decade of the square being built in 1670 every single house was lived in by someone who had a title or was sleeping with someone with a title.

But what makes the square really interesting is the bizarre statue of William III in the gardens. The statue is only here because the residents got fed up with the fact that the centre of the square was long used as a refuse tip for the householders – at one time it was piled high with 'kitchen rubbish, dead cats, scraps of timber and noxious mountains of refuse'. They wanted something to give the middle a purpose and a statue seemed as good an idea as anything. But that's where the problems began.

The idea of a statue of William was not initially popular so despite their enormous wealth the residents of the square refused to pay for it. Then a merchant offered money in his will but his family contested the will for the next seventy years and it wasn't until 1806 that the statue was finally completed.

Even when the statue was finally made and put on its plinth there was something odd about it – it includes, for example, a small molehill at the feet of the horse on which William is seated. What is the molehill for?

The answer is that William is said to have died after falling from his horse. The horse had tripped on a molehill.

William was the Protestant king brought to England from Holland to replace the last Catholic, King James. James's supporters and all Jacobites then and now still toast the little gentleman in velvet – i.e. the mole that built the molehill that killed a king.

THE DIRTIEST PUB IN LONDON

1809

Many London pubs are far older than they might at first appear. In Bishopsgate, for example, Dirty Dicks dates back to the early eighteenth century despite the fact that the pub looks typically mid-Victorian. The cellars here are original and it was in the pub above them that one of London's most extraordinary and eccentric characters once lived.

The story varies in its details but it seems that Nathaniel Bentley, a local businessman and dandy who ran an alehouse, decided to get married. Everything was prepared and the pub's dining rooms had been laid out with beautiful flowers, cutlery, linen and a huge cake, but on the night before the wedding the bride died. Distraught, Bentley sealed up the room where the table had been laid for the wedding breakfast and never opened it again. He also stopped washing and only changed his clothes when they rotted and fell off him. He allowed his pub to become one of the filthiest houses in London but people flocked to it to see if it really was as bad as they'd been told and Bentley made a fortune – a fortune he never spent because he bought nothing. He lived for nearly forty years, and died finally in 1809. He was a rich man by then. He once said: 'What is the point of washing my hands or anything else for that matter when they will only be dirty again tomorrow?'

The remnants of the old clothes that hung from the ceiling were only cleared out (they fell foul of new health and safety rules) in the 1980s, but the old pub still has a few fake rags here and there to remind us of its decidedly grubby past.

NAPOLEON'S SOAP ON SHOW

1816

It's hard to understand now, but despite the fact that he was defeated at Waterloo the Emperor Napoleon was one of the most popular figures in London at the beginning of the nineteenth century – popular in the sense that people were absolutely fascinated by everything to do with him now that he was safely imprisoned on the island of St Helena.

The great bogeyman of Europe who had terrified the British ruling classes (they thought he would encourage the lower orders to get above themselves) was now like a lion in a cage – awe-inspiring but harmless.

Napoleon fever reached a peak in around 1816 when the showman William Bullock bought a vast collection of Napoleon's personal effects – the collection included Napoleon's carriage, his horses, his combs, brushes, wine, spirits and even a small bar of his soap!

Even more extraordinary was the fact that Bullock managed to persuade Napoleon's former carriage driver to accompany the collection. It was all brought to Bullock's new British Museum, which was situated in Piccadilly, and within a few months almost half a million people had queued to see the collection. Bullock made a fortune and the British appetite for sensation was satisfied.

In fact Bullock did so well that he moved his collection of Napoleon artifacts into what he called the Museum Napoleon. But the obsession with the fallen Emperor didn't end there – a forty square metre replica of the battlefield at Waterloo was created at the Egyptian Hall in Piccadilly with every detail, soldiers, artillery, horses and landmarks included.

HOW TO STOP DEAD CATS FLYING

1819

One of the delights of London is that if you know what you are looking for you will find odd, quirky little places in the busiest thoroughfares and many of these have fascinating and often curious histories. Piccadilly must be one of the most famous streets in the world, but just off it is a row of tiny Georgian shops virtually unchanged since they were completed in 1819.

The shops in question are in the Burlington Arcade and they are here for a most bizarre reason. Visitors often think the Georgian planners who built these little shops were simply building to make a profit. In fact they built the arcade to cover a narrow alley that ran alongside Burlington House, now the home of the Royal Academy but in the early nineteenth century still a private home. The owner of Burlington House was Lord George Cavendish, who had complained for years that while sitting in his garden he was constantly hit on the head by oyster shells, apple cores, old bottles and even an occasional dead cat. These unpleasant items were thrown over the wall between the garden and the lane which then existed at its side. Cavendish decided that a row of shops would put paid to the nuisance and so he had them built and the alleyway vanished forever. Samuel Ware was asked to design the beautiful shop fronts which exist largely unchanged today, and though the shop interiors are tiny the shopkeepers have always sold luxury goods, so what they lack in quantity of stock they more than make up for in quality.

Originally the arcade was a single storey, but an upper level was added in 1906 and above the shops the rooms were let – according to one wag they were let to 'the better sort of courtesan'. The beautiful triple-arch entrance was destroyed for no good reason in 1931 and the new design was much hated. There was also some damage during the war but the arcade remains one of the world's first shopping malls. Instead of security men it still has a beadle who will ask you to leave the arcade if he catches you running or whistling or carrying an open umbrella!

THE GREATEST LEGAL
SCANDAL OF ALL

1819

The law has always been something of a scandalous institution. Lawyers have the best trade union in the sense that entry to the profession is strictly controlled and because lawyers never undercut each other and there is no genuine competition between practitioners, the poor public is always forced to pay very high prices for the advice it receives.

But the scandal of lawyers' costs today – a disgrace that no government dares tackle simply because politicians themselves tend to be drawn from the ranks of the legal profession – is nothing compared with the scandals of the past.

One of the greatest and most extraordinary of all legal humiliations, a scandal that outranks every other London legal dishonour, was known as the Great Jennings case.

Anyone who has read Charles Dickens's great novel of London life *Bleak House* will remember the case of Jarndyce and Jarndyce, which is the central symbol in that novel of social decay and corruption.

The case of Jarndyce and Jarndyce, though bizarre in its tortuousness, impenetrability and sheer longevity, was based on the Great Jennings case which was heard in the Old Hall, Lincoln's Inn. The real case was no less absurd than the story Dickens created to satirise it.

The Great Jennings case started in 1819 when Dickens was only seven and didn't end until 1870, the year in which the great novelist died. But why was the case such a scandal? The answer is that the lawyers involved made no real efforts to conclude it; it was in their interest to keep it going as long as possible only because they were earning fat fees. The case finally ended when the money involved in the case ran out – it had all been used up funding lawyers' fees.

A CLUB FOR MEN NOT ABLE TO SING IN THE BATH

1820

Old pubs tend to survive longer than other buildings in London – with the exception of churches, of course. The Coal Hole in Carting Lane is a case in point. The present building dates back to the early 1800s but the pub commemorates an earlier nearby tavern of the same name.

The pub gets its name from the wharf used by coalmen that stood nearby before the Embankment pushed the river further away. For centuries coal was brought to London by ship from the mines of Northumberland and Durham (which is why in earlier centuries coal was always called sea coal) and the tough city coal heavers who lugged the sacks from the ships uphill to the carters liked to drink in this pub.

During the eighteenth century the pub was hugely popular with actors and theatre managers including the great tragedian Edmund Kean (1787–1833), who started the Wolf Club.

The sole qualification for membership was that the applicant should have been forbidden by his wife to sing in the bath! The Wolf Bar in the present attractive Arts and Crafts interior with its pretty leaded windows commemorates this bizarre drinking club. And when you step out of the pub you can still look down the sloping lane and see the bright river – just as the coal heavers of earlier centuries did.

TOM AND JERRY IN LONDON

1821

If they think about them at all, most people probably imagine that the famous cartoon characters Tom and Jerry have their origin in the United States and more particularly in the vast film industry of that country.

In fact Tom and Jerry have their origins far earlier and on the other side of the Atlantic. The story starts in 1821 – well within the Georgian era – when London was enjoying a boom in publishing. Books, pamphlets and newspapers were being produced in ever greater numbers as literacy and the appetite for reading material spread through society.

A century earlier books had been largely the preserve of the rich or at least the comparatively well off, but by 1821 the popular press had taken off with a vengeance – in addition to cheap pamphlets and books there were broadsides (single news sheets usually about murders and executions) song sheets, chapbooks and penny dreadfuls.

Among the most innovative of the new publishers was Pierce Egan (1772–1849), a sporting journalist, who began a new series of publications in 1821 entitled *Life in London or the Day and Night Scenes of Jerry Hawthorne Esq and his elegant friend Corinthian Tom, accompanied by Bob Logic, the Oxonian, in their Rambles and Sprees Through the Metropolis.*

The series was so popular that other publishers produced pirated versions of it and within a few months it had been turned into a stage play – the title had changed by now to *Tom and Jerry or Life in London* but it was so popular and tripped so easily off the tongue that it is not difficult to see how it crossed the Atlantic in the head of some entrepreneur emigré and ended up transformed into the cartoon we know today. The basic idea of two characters getting into a series of scrapes remains the same but Egan's loveable human rogues have been transformed, of course, into a cat and a mouse.

WHEN THE DEAD MOVED OUT OF LONDON

1832

Most visitors brave enough to include a graveyard on their London itinerary go to Highgate cemetery to the north of the city, but tucked away by the side of the Grand Union Canal over to the west in what was until recently a fairly poor part of North Kensington, Kensal Green Cemetery is an extraordinary monument to Victorian funeral piety – and even more bizarre funeral rituals.

Until the coming of the canal in the eighteenth century this was a quiet place: there were a few houses at the junction of Harrow Road and Kilburn Lane but the rest was open farmland with an odd isolated inn and London half a day's walk away. But by the early 1800s the small village centred round the junction and its green was expanding. By the 1830s London's church graveyards were filled to bursting and All Soul's Cemetery, as Kensal Green Cemetery was originally known (the land was owned by All Souls College, Oxford), was opened in 1832 to ease the problem.

Within a few years Kensal Rise Cemetery – as it quickly became known – was the fashionable place to be buried. Among the bizarre monuments the cemetery contains are Greek temples, Egyptian halls, gothic fantasies and medieval castles, as well as more ordinary but equally fascinating gravestones and tombs.

The cemetery is full of mature trees and shrubs and gives every indication of being deep in the heart of the countryside – among the tombs to look out for are those of Sir Anthony Panizzi (1797–1879), who created the famous round Reading Room at the British Library (now part of the British Museum), Charles Babbage (1791–1871) who created the first computer, authors Wilkie Collins (1824–1889), William Makepeace Thackeray (1811–1863) and Anthony Trollope (1815–1882), as well as the greatest of all the Victorian engineers, Isambard Kingdom Brunel (1806–1859).

But Kensal Rise Cemetery has a strange secret – here and there are tombs that reveal an astonishing obsession that gripped Victorian Londoners for several decades. And what was this obsession? It was the fear of being buried alive.

From roughly 1870 until 1900 an idea grew up that doctors were constantly making mistakes when it came to deciding when a person had died. It was said that in many cases death certificates had been issued and the body was being prepared for laying out, when suddenly an eye flickered or the apparent corpse groaned. If a corpse could come back to life at this stage, who was to say that dozens – perhaps hundreds – had not been buried and only then come back to life?

Visitors to Highgate and Kensal Green cemeteries in London even today may see the remnants of a strange invention designed to guard against the risk of being buried on Monday and waking up in one's coffin on Wednesday. A number of tombs were built with a hollow stone column running down into the buried coffin. At the top of the hollow column two or three feet up in the air above the tombstone would be a small bell tower complete with bell.

The idea of the bizarre contraption was that if the deceased happened to wake up after burial he or she would be able to pull vigorously on a chain that ran up the hollow column to the bell, which would ring out, bringing rescuers hotfooting it across the fields.

A number of different coffin alarm systems were created around this time and, indeed, from then until well into the twentieth century, when in a few cases nervous relatives had electric alarms fitted to their relatives' coffins.

Despite all the terror and fears, however, there is no record of anyone buried with an alarm pressing the button or ringing the bell.

THE MAN WHO HAD HIMSELF STUFFED

1832

In earlier epochs the belief in the resurrection of the body – central to Christianity – meant that cremation was frowned on as a means of disposing of the dead. By the eighteenth century, in England at least, such ideas were being questioned and among the rationalists of the Enlightenment arguments about cremation versus burial came to seem absurd. It may well have been partly why the philosopher Jeremy Bentham (1748–1832), one of the great political and social thinkers of the later eighteenth and early nineteenth centuries, came up with a rather more unusual way of disposing of his own corpse.

Bentham's more than sixty published works cover everything from the need for political reform to animal welfare, discussions of the state of the colonies and the evils of swearing. Most famously, of course, he is associated with the creation of utilitarianism – the doctrine of the greatest good of the greatest number. He was also closely involved in the whole idea of a dissenters' university, which is what the University of London originally was. Dissenters were not allowed to study at the old universities so they set up their own. Bentham was considered wildly eccentric in his day for advocating universal suffrage and the decriminalisation of homosexuality.

The University of London started life in 1828 when Bentham was in his eighties and though he took no practical part in establishing it he is often considered its spiritual father, largely because of his advocacy of religious tolerance and education for all. Bentham loved the new university so it should come as no surprise that he left the university (later to become University College London) all his manuscripts. But he also left a legacy of surpassing eccentricity. Visitors to the South Cloisters of the main building cannot fail to see the large wooden and glass cabinet that stands in the corridor.

Inside the cabinet is a surprisingly lifelike and life-size Jeremy Bentham, comfortably seated with a stick in his hand and dressed in the very clothes he wore in life. The figure is not a model but the actual preserved remains of the great man. It was Bentham's last joke, if you like, at the expense of those who argued over burial and cremation for superstitious (i.e. religious) reasons.

When Bentham first arrived in his case a few weeks after his death in 1832, the head and face were actually those of Bentham, but the embalming technique used wasn't up to scratch and the head deteriorated badly until a wax replica had to be made. Bentham had left his body to the college on condition that it was preserved in this way and beneath the clothing even today Bentham's skeleton keeps an eye on the academic world he so loved in life.

Legends and extraordinary stories about the preserved philosopher abound – one says that he is wheeled into every university council meeting. At the end of each meeting the minutes record: Jeremy Bentham – present but not voting. Another legend has it that for a decade before he died Bentham carried around the glass eyes he wanted used in his preserved head. When they were finally used in the preserved head they fell out; then the head itself fell off and was found between Bentham's feet. Whatever the truth or otherwise of these and many other stories (including the one about the students found playing football with the head) we do know that in fact the real head is kept in the college vaults.

No one knows precisely why Bentham stipulated in his will that he should be preserved and set up for public display in this way, but it ties in nicely with the philosophy of a man who took a practical view of affairs and who thought it was important to make a contribution to the day-to-day life of the society in which he lived – at the end of his life he probably thought it would be nice to be in some position where he could watch the world go by and it was good to cock a snook at the more religious among his colleagues who were outraged at this refusal to stick to the Christian rules about the dead. No doubt Bentham also thought that if there was anything in the stories about the survival of the soul then his could hover where it had been happiest – in the corridors of the university.

WHY THE NATIONAL GALLERY HAS GIANT PEPPERPOTS

1835

When the National Gallery was built the architect found himself in a tricky position. His brief was to build something long and very narrow, as the access road behind the site (which is still there today) had to remain as it was when the royal stables, or mews, was here.

Not only that but, in a typically English and eccentric fudge, he also had to agree to build his new gallery no higher than the mews buildings it replaced. The idea was that the skyline at this point should look pretty much as it had done since the Middle Ages when the Royal Mews, a little to the north of the Palace of Westminster, was first established. The mews was where the king's animals – particularly his falcons – were 'mewed up'.

The architect of the National Gallery, as good as his word, came up with the design we see today and the oddest echo of the building the gallery replaced can be seen at either end of the present building. If you look carefully at the roof there are what look like two stone pepperpots, one at either end of the structure.

The reason these are here is that the original stables had almost identical decorative pepperpots – the originals were actually part of the ventilation system for the stables. As the heat and smell of the dung of several hundred horses rose it had to be dispersed from the building as quickly as possible – the pepperpots with their open stone latticework allowed just that to happen and the replacement pepperpots on the building have the same open decorative latticework, despite the fact that the horses departed forever nearly two centuries ago.

WORLD'S SMALLEST PRISON

1835

At one time most English towns and villages had lock-ups – small single-celled buildings where local drunks might be kept secure for the night or where thieves or other antisocial individuals could be kept to await the arrival of the magistrate.

At the southeast corner of Trafalgar Square and missed by almost every tourist who comes to this place is a lock-up that is unique even by the standards of these odd little prisons, because the Trafalgar Square lock-up is also Britain's (possibly the world's) smallest police station.

The structure looks like a rather fat lamppost and it is only when one looks closely that one notices the tiny door and window. There is barely room for two people to stand upright inside but it is said that this tiny lock-up had and still has a direct telephone link to Scotland Yard.

Right up until the 1960s the Trafalgar Square lock-up was still in use, but it is by no means the only strange thing about this part of London.

Take the famous lions at the bottom of Nelson's Column, for example. When the column was being built an artist had to be found to design the four huge lions round the base of the column. They are so much bigger than life size that it was feared the final result would be embarrassingly out of proportion unless someone with the right talents was chosen to complete the work.

Queen Victoria wanted Edwin Landseer (1862–1873), one of her favourite painters, to carry out the work but Landseer was horrified at the suggestion. He was not a sculptor and had no useful experience to bring to bear. He refused the commission, but the Queen would not give up. After being approached by peers and MPs, Landseer finally agreed but only on condition that he could take as long as he needed and that a dead lion would be sent round to his studio so he could study it before putting pen to paper.

It took several months before a lion died (presumably of natural causes) at London Zoo. It was immediately sent round to Landseer's house where he kept it until it stank so badly the neighbours began to complain. It took more than a year of preparatory drawing (and several more dead lions) before Landseer was finally happy – and the result was the splendid lions we see today.

But a century and more ago nothing seemed quite so straightforward – the drawings were ready but the sculpted lions were not installed until 25 years after they should have been put up. When Landseer died wreaths were draped around the lions' necks as a mark of respect.

Another curious tale concerns the capital at the top of the column on which Nelson's statue stands and the bronze bas-reliefs at the bottom of the column showing Nelson's victories (as well as his yet more famous death). All are made from French cannons captured after the Battle of Trafalgar in 1805.

TRAFALGAR SQUARE – PERMANENTLY UNFINISHED

1838

Present-day Trafalgar Square is built on the site where Henry VIII and earlier kings once kept their birds of prey and their horses. The site was first built on when Chaucer was Clerk of the King's Works in the 1380s and Richard II needed somewhere close to the rambling Palace of Whitehall for the royal hawks. Gradually the word mews was used not just for hawks and falcons but for other animals kept either for royal use or entertainment. The royal mews lasted well beyond the destruction by fire of the Palace of Westminster but the area in which the mews stood gradually became a warren of small dirty lanes where 'thieves and vagabonds abound', but by the time the area (by then known as the Bermudas) was cleared completely to allow for the building of the present square the word 'mews' had passed into the language and meant any narrow alleyway where horses were kept. Today in Belgravia and Mayfair the narrow back lanes behind grand house are still often called mews, for here the servants lived in small cottages or above the stables where their employers' horses were kept.

Like most building projects in London, Trafalgar Square was the subject of endless disputes and arguments – the plans for the National Gallery (completed in 1838) were derided by many who thought the proposed building an architectural disaster.

But unlike most projects, which are eventually built and completed, however greatly modified during the planning process, Trafalgar Square has never been completed and remains unfinished to this day.

The unfinished bit is the empty plinth in the northwest corner – this has been empty ever since the square was first built and though in recent years some bizarre sculptures have been placed on the unused plinth (including an upside-down see-through version of the plinth itself!) there are still no plans to erect a permanent statue here.

THE MYSTERIOUS CROSSING SWEEPER

1840

It's easy to forget that London's streets were, until comparatively recently, completely uncared for. In Victorian times many streets were cobbled, or were made from wooden sets (blocks of wood packed tightly with their end-grain uppermost to reduce wear) but elsewhere they were entirely unmade. In poorer districts the population would still throw their slops into the street just as their medieval ancestors did. And of course everywhere was the dung left by thousands of horses. But the mess in the streets had one great advantage – it produced jobs for hundreds if not thousands of London's poorest citizens. These were the crossing sweepers. Perhaps the most famous crossing sweeper – a trade that vanished with the coming of the motor car – was Jo in Charles Dickens's novel *Bleak House*. Jo was Dickens's attempt to show how damaging it was to society as a whole to allow children to live the sort of life Jo lives. Illiterate, half-dressed even in winter and forced to sleep in the streets, Jo earns a few pennies each day by sweeping a path through the horse manure from one side of a London street to another. Many destitute men, women and children were forced to do this work simply because they had nothing else, but one of the most remarkable stories of a crossing sweeper concerns a real-life sweeper called Brutus Billy or Charles McGhee.

Nothing is known of McGhee's history, but he was an elderly black man who had probably come to England from the West Indies.

For many years in the early nineteenth century he swept a path across Fleet Street where it meets Ludgate Hill near a wealthy linen draper's shop in Fleet Street. The shop was owned by Robert Waithman who later became MP for the City of London. From the window above the shop the draper's daughter watched the old crossing sweeper and on cold days she arranged for someone to take him a bowl of hot soup and some bread. When McGhee died some years later it was discovered that he had left all his savings – some £700, which was an extraordinary sum in Victorian times – to the draper's daughter.

A BRIDGE FROM LONDON
TO BRISTOL

1845

The Clifton Suspension Bridge is one of the wonders of nineteenth-century engineering, but one of the strangest things about it – a fact that is almost forgotten today – is that it started life in central London.

The story begins with the decision by the Earl of Hungerford to build a fruit and vegetable market to rival the one at Covent Garden. Hungerford market began life in 1692 on the site now occupied by Charing Cross Station but it never came to rival Covent Garden, the more famous market down the road. An attempt to improve things – by bringing customers in from south of the river – came when Isambard Kingdom Brunel built Hungerford Suspension Bridge in 1845.

Hungerford market finally disappeared when the railway company bought the land and built Charing Cross Station, but they too needed a bridge over the river and it would have to carry trains.

Before the current walkways were built, the railway company sold the old suspension bridge to the city of Bristol and then built their new railway bridge – in the strict legal sense there are still two bridges here, which may explain why on some maps the existing bridge is referred to as Hungerford Bridge while others insist on calling it Charing Cross Bridge. The reason is that the London public had got used to being able to cross the bridge and the railway company's plan would have deprived them of their old crossing because the new bridge would have been used by trains only. The railway company was forced by public pressure to build its railway bridge with a pedestrian footbridge alongside, which is why today the railway bridge into Charing Cross Station is the only railway bridge in London that also has a pedestrian footbridge. The pedestrian footbridge is Hungerford Bridge, while the railway bridge alongside is Charing Cross Bridge.

WHY BIG BEN ISN'T BIG BEN AT ALL

1852

Big Ben is one of London's oddest buildings and the story of how it came to be built is typical of the eccentric way in which things tend to get done in London. Like the rest of the Palace of Westminster, it was built by Charles Barry (1795–1860) and Augustus Pugin (1812–1852) after a nationwide competition to find a new design for the seat of government after the disastrous fire of 1834.

The late Georgian passion for Gothic gave the Barry design a head start and after duly winning the competition, he began building the clock tower we see today, but when it was first built it wasn't known as Big Ben at all – the name Big Ben refers to the huge bell on which the hours are struck.

All the statistics to do with St Stephen's Tower (as Big Ben is really known) and its great clock are astonishing: the tower is nearly three hundred and twenty feet high; it took almost nineteen years from laying the first foundation stone to getting the clock going, largely because no one could agree about who should make it.

The job was first offered to Benjamin Vulliamy, the Queen's clockmaker, who was based in Pall Mall. His design was attacked as absurd and incompetent by another clockmaker, J. Dent, and after a huge fight with letters banging to and fro and *Times* leaders thundering out various opinions, the commissioners charged with organising the work gave in and launched a competition to design and build the new clock.

The contract finally went to Dent amid much acrimony, in 1852. Two years later the unique clock – fifteen and a half feet long by nearly five feet wide – was ready, but there was nowhere to put it because wrangles over the building of the tower had delayed construction.

While all this was being sorted out, an east London company cast a great sixteen-ton bell, but during tests using a thirteen-hundredweight clapper the bell cracked. It then had to be melted down and recast, this time by the Whitechapel Bell foundry. It took sixteen horses the best part of a day to haul the gigantic bell to Parliament Square. It was then hoisted into position at the top of the tower, which was completed just in time.

When the clock began to run it was discovered that the two and a half ton hands were so heavy that the mechanism could not move them. They were redesigned in a lighter metal but now crashed down past the three each time they reached 12. Remade for a third time in hollow copper, they worked and they have kept time accurately ever since.

There are two theories about the origins of the name 'Big Ben': around the time the clock was due to be completed, the prizefighter and publican Ben Caunt went sixty rounds with the best bare-knuckle boxer in the country, Nat Langham. The bout was declared a draw but it made both men national heroes. Ben Caunt was a huge man and one story has it that the great bell was named after him. The other story attributes the name to Benjamin Hall, the chief commissioner of works, who was addressing the House on the subject of a name for the new bell tower when, to great laughter, someone shouted 'Call it Big Ben!'

Perhaps the most remarkable thing about the clock is that even by the standards of today's atomic timepieces it is wonderfully accurate. When the commissioners launched their competition to design it they stipulated that it must be accurate to within one second an hour – most clock makers at the time agreed that this was impossible but that's how accurate the clock still is today. If it does get slightly out of time, a tiny coin, kept especially for the purpose, is placed on the huge pendulum and the weight of the coin is enough to adjust the clock by a fraction of a second.

TRAINS ONLY FOR THE DEAD

1854

Just outside Waterloo Station between what was once York Street (it was recently renamed Leake Street) and the Westminster Bridge Road is a curious reddish building with a grey-stone arched entranceway. This is the former entrance to one of London's most extraordinary railway stations.

The current building dates from the early twentieth century but it replaced a station building opened on the same site in 1854. The station was the London terminus for the Necropolis Railway – a railway devoted entirely to the dead.

To find out how this bizarre situation came about we have to remember that by the mid-nineteenth century London's churchyards were full to overflowing. Bodies were stamped down into graves already too full and in many cases just a few inches of soil covered the decaying corpses. The result was appallingly insanitary conditions and frequent outbreaks of disease.

To ease the problems London's churchyards were closed and building began on a number of out-of-town cemeteries – Kensal Green and, more famously, Highgate. South of London, Brookwood Cemetery was opened some 25 miles from London, but the great difficulty was how to get corpse, coffin and mourners there. The solution was the Necropolis Railway.

Funeral trains ran from what was really a private station attached to the main line. Once out of the station the funeral trains joined the main line until they reached Brookwood. Here they reversed into the grounds of the cemetery. Until 1902 when the station was rebuilt following the complete rebuilding of the rest of Waterloo Station, Necropolis trains ran every day if there was a booking. After 1900, for some inexplicable reason, trains ceased to run on Sundays and a few years later they were running no more than twice a week. In 1941 the station was bombed (the façade survived) and the funeral trains were never revived after the war.

In the late 1940s the track from London to Brookwood was taken up but the station and track survived in the grounds of Brookwood Cemetery for a little longer. There were two stations in the cemetery – the north station served Nonconformists and the south station served the Anglican dead. The north station was demolished in the early 1960s but the south station survived until a fire in 1972. Today, the remains of the station platforms can still be seen at Brookwood – the only reminder of the thousands of dead who took their last journey on the Necropolis railway.

HOW TO MAKE A LIVING
SELLING DOG POO

1861

Poverty in earlier centuries pushed tens of thousands of Londoners into very peculiar occupations – peculiar at least by modern standards. There was a huge market for live birds, for example, and this market was met by hundreds of live-bird sellers who might walk twenty miles out of London to catch a dozen or so birds before walking the twenty miles back again. They would then repeat this journey three or four times a week.

Or take the mudlarks who scoured the river foreshore at low tide. They went barefoot whatever the weather, searching for copper nails from the ships, for old bottles – anything in fact that they might be able to sell.

The toshers, on the other hand, were men who risked their lives searching for valuables in London's vast, unmapped warren of sewers. Toshers tended to be from the same few families and they handed down their knowledge of the sewer network from generation to generation, but even generations of experience couldn't always protect them and many died when sudden rainfall flooded the system or the lamps and candles they carried were blown out or they were overcome by gas.

But perhaps the strangest job of all was that of the pure finder – a job that existed, perhaps could only have existed, in Victorian London.

A pure finder was someone who spent his days searching for dog faeces to sell to leather tanners, particularly to those tanners engaged in producing leather for the bookbinding trade.

Henry Mayhew's extraordinary book *London Labour and the London Poor* charts the lives of a number of pure finders. Mayhew explains that in the 1830s and 1840s only women seem to have been involved in the trade and they were known as 'bunters'. By the 1850s, when Mayhew carried out his research, men, women and children were working as pure finders. Pure finders sold the dog faeces they collected for roughly ten old pence a bucketful. The tanners – mostly based in Bermondsey (where thirty tanneries are recorded in the 1860s) – preferred the dry sort of faeces as it contained more alkaline and it was the alkaline that worked its magic on the leather.

Curiously, Mayhew and others recorded that many of the pure finders were well-educated men and women who had fallen on hard times. His description of the trade is hugely evocative:

The pure-finder is often found in the open streets, as dogs wander where they like. The pure-finders always carry a handle basket, generally with a cover, to hide the contents, and have their right hand covered with a black leather glove; many of them, however, dispense with the glove, as they say it is much easier to wash their hands than to keep the glove fit for use. The women generally have a large pocket for the reception of such rags as they may chance to fall in with, but they pick up those only of the very best quality, and will not go out of their way to search even for them. Thus equipped they may be seen pursuing their avocation in almost every street in and about London, excepting such streets as are now cleansed by the street orderlies, of whom the pure-finders grievously complain, as being an unwarrantable interference with the privileges of their class.

The pure collected is used by leather-dressers and tanners, and more especially by those engaged in the manufacture of morocco and kid leather from the skins of old and young goats, of which skins great numbers are imported, and of the roans and lambskins which are the sham morocco and kids of the slop leather trade, and are used by the better class of shoemakers, book binders, and glovers, for the inferior requirements of their business. Pure is also used by tanners, as is pigeons' dung, for the tanning of the thinner kinds of leather, such as calf-skins, for which purpose it is placed in pits with an admixture of lime and bark.

In the manufacture of moroccos and roans the pure is rubbed by the hands of the workman into the skin he is dressing. This is done to purify the leather, I was told by an intelligent leatherdresser, and from that term the word pure has originated. The dung has astringent as well as highly alkaline, or, to use the expression of my informant, scouring, qualities. When the pure has been rubbed into the flesh and grain of the skin (the flesh being originally the interior, and the grain the exterior part of the cuticle), and the skin, thus purified, has been hung up to be dried, the dung removes, as it were, all such moisture as, if allowed to remain, would tend to make the leather unsound or imperfectly dressed. This imperfect dressing, moreover, gives a disagreeable smell to the leather and leather-buyers often use both nose and tongue in making their purchases...

WHERE IS THE CENTRE OF LONDON?

1865

One of the oddest things about London is that most people have no idea where it begins – or more precisely where its centre actually is. Many think that the statue of Eros in Piccadilly Circus marks the centre point; others are convinced that Buckingham Palace marks the spot, or St Paul's Cathedral.

In fact – and for the strangest reason – the centre of London is located at a spot just behind the equestrian statue of Charles I at the southern edge of Trafalgar Square. If you look carefully there is a brass plate in the roadway that marks the precise spot.

But what adds to the oddity of this is that strictly speaking – and despite modern rearrangements to suit the traffic – the brass plate set in the ground here is not in Trafalgar Square at all. It is Charing Cross. The Charing Cross we see today – which is outside the Charing Cross railway hotel just a few hundred yards away – was put up in 1865 as a publicity stunt to attract attention to the new railway terminus.

The medieval Charing Cross from which the area gets its name was actually at the top of Whitehall where the brass plaque is now.

But why choose this exact spot to define the centre of London? The answer has to do with the bizarre growth of the capital – to the east of the plaque is the City of London; to the south Westminster.

Edward the Confessor (1003–1066) made a vow to go on a pilgrimage to Rome, but domestic unrest made this impossible and he sought absolution from his vow by promising to build a huge church. He chose Thorney Island for his church – a small area of high ground above the surrounding marsh of the Thames. This area – we now call it Westminster – already had a small monastery, but Edward enlarged it considerably and added Westminster Abbey, the church we see today. The new church was complete by 1065.

The merchants of the City had no intention of moving to what was then a windswept and remote location so they stayed put, but when the legislators at Westminster Hall wanted to hear news of the commercial goings on of the City they came to the halfway point – Charing Cross – and the City merchants wanting to know more of affairs of state also came to this spot.

The brass plaque marks the exact halfway point between the old city and the new seat of government and is therefore the centre point, as it were, of both Londons.

With the growth of the civil service in the nineteenth and twentieth centuries the brass plaque helped solve a more practical problem too: where London weighting was paid to public officials there had to be a decision about the area of London within which the extra rate of pay would be calculated. It was decided that anyone working within a six-mile radius of the brass plaque at Charing Cross would be entitled to the extra payment.

THE HOUSES THAT EXIST BUT AREN'T THERE

1868

An elegant stuccoed street in Paddington hides one of the oddest pairs of houses in the world. The passer-by would hardly notice that numbers 23 and 24 Leinster Gardens have permanently darkened windows, nor that the front doors have a curiously solid feel to them. But look closely and you quickly realise that these are not actually houses at all.

The story starts in the 1860s when the world's first underground railway was being constructed. The Metropolitan line – which was opened in 1868 – was built on the cut and cover principle. This meant that to build a tunnel you first had to dig a huge trench. Once this was done the circular supports (to make the tunnel) were fitted and the whole then covered with earth again. When the line between Bayswater and Paddington was being built it became necessary to demolish two houses in what was then a recently built and highly prestigious row of terraced houses.

Numerous railway acts tended to ride roughshod over the rights of tenants and landlords in the mid-Victorian era so the railway company simply compulsorily purchased two houses in the path of their tunnel and knocked them down. But the householders on either side refused to be beaten by a mere Act of Parliament – they managed to force through a condition that when the tunnel had been built and covered over, the facades at least of the two demolished houses should be reinstated.

And that is precisely what happened. What look like a pair of rather grand houses are actually only walls about five feet thick.

If you retrace your steps from Leinster Gardens to Porchester Road, which runs parallel to Leinster Gardens, you come to a long wall. Look over this and you will see the backs of 23 and 24 Leinster Gardens – a high, blank brick wall held up by steel girders. Below the wall is the tunnel entrance. But this is only a short stretch of exposed railway and it could have been covered over. The reason it is still open to the skies is that the first underground railway trains were steam driven and though they were specially adapted to reduce steam and smoke emissions in the tunnels (which would have been very unhealthy for passengers) they did have to release large amounts of coal exhaust fumes now and then. The spot behind the fake houses was established as an acceptable place for those early drivers to vent their engines!

A ROAR ON THE EMBANKMENT

1870

The Thames has always dominated life in London – the City's huge wealth was built on trade via the river and for centuries most people travelled across London by water as the roads were almost always either cluttered or deep in mud or both.

London was in constant danger of flooding too and even today, with the Thames Barrier in place, rising sea levels could threaten the city again.

The real problem with flooding when the embankment walls were built was that, despite the great height of the embankment walls, they had the effect of narrowing the river and increasing its depth. Add to that the fact that nothing could control the great surges that began far out at sea and then drove remorselessly upriver. When heavy rain in winter coincided with a big spring tide the embankment was often breached in numerous places, causing tens of thousands of pounds of damage to property, not to mention disruption to transport and people's lives generally.

There was, however, a bizarre and rather primitive early warning system that is still partially in use today.

Anyone who has ever leaned over the embankment to gaze out along the river will probably have noticed that well below the parapet and fixed at regular intervals into the stonework there are lions' heads with mooring rings hanging from their mouths. Visitors often wonder why on earth so many mooring positions should be required so far below the top of the wall – the passengers of any boat tying up at any of these rings could not possibly disembark.

The solution to this mystery is tied up with the early warning system for flooding that existed in London before the Thames Barrier was built.

Every policeman whose beat happens to take him along the embankment on either side of the river was formerly instructed to keep an eye on the lions' heads, because if the water level reaches the heads flooding is a serious and imminent danger. The rule used to be that once the water reached the heads all Underground stations were closed and London was put on red alert.

THE HOUSE WHERE TIME STOOD STILL

1874

There is a common misconception that London is still a wonderful place to find eighteenth- and early nineteenth-century architecture despite the deadly work of redevelopers and German bombs, but actually the majority of eighteenth-century houses are only eighteenth century in outward appearance. Only a few rare examples are listed in such a way as to prevent their interiors being destroyed, even if their facades have to be left unchanged. This means that thousands of modern houses and office blocks have eighteenth-century fronts. This even happened – back in the 1960s – to houses of great architectural merit – like Schomberg House in Pall Mall, a beautiful seventeenth-century house that developers were allowed to destroy so long as they kept the façade. Great houses and churches often survive with their interiors but the least likely to survive of all are the interiors of the houses of the middle and working classes.

Linley Sambourne House is an extraordinary exception to that rule. Named after the cartoonist who lived here from 1874 to 1910, it is a perfect example of a solidly middle-class household of the mid-Victorian period. When Sambourne and his young wife moved into the house, which had been built only four years earlier, they decorated in the then fashionable aesthetic style – characterised by heavy velvet drapes, William Morris wallpapers, ornate Turkey carpets and a vast clutter of china ornaments.

Sambourne earned his living as a cartoonist, mostly for *Punch* magazine, for almost half a century. Most of his drawings were completed in this house and numerous examples of his work can be seen, along with his photographs – like many artists of the time he was fascinated by this still relatively new art form.

The house remained substantially unchanged through the twentieth century through extraordinary good luck. The Sambournes' son Roy inherited the house and left it unchanged, probably because he never married. When he in turn died he left the house to his elder sister Maud. She too was passionate about preserving it intact, largely because – as she said herself – she'd been so happy there as a child. Her daughter Anne then used the house until at a party in 1957 Anne proposed that she and her friends, including the future Poet Laureate John Betjeman (1906–1984), should found the Victorian Society to preserve the house and its contents and to work for the preservation of other similar examples of Victorian taste. The Victorian style was then hugely unpopular – how unpopular can be judged by the fact that sometime in the mid-1950s Lord Leighton's famous painting 'Hope', now one of the most popular works in the collection of pictures at Tate Britain, was used to block up an old fireplace in a house in Battersea!

A NEEDLE BY THE RIVER

1878

Londoners have never allowed the truth to get in the way of a good story, which is why Cleopatra's Needle – that ancient Egyptian monument on London's Embankment – has always retained a name that has nothing to do with reality.

But then everything about Cleopatra's Needle is bizarre. Like most Egyptian artifacts its history is uncertain, but the most likely date for it is around 1500 BC. It was almost certainly commissioned by Thothmes III, whose name appears on the stone. By the year 23 BC it had been moved by Caesar to a position near Cleopatra's Palace, but that is as far as any connection with the great empress goes.

After that it vanishes from history until early in the nineteenth century when it was presented by the local Egyptian ruler as a gift to King George IV. It arrived in London in 1878 after a long campaign to raise enough money to cover the cost of transporting it.

The cost was enormous because the stone is incredibly heavy – 160 tons – and a special case had to be made to move it without damaging it.

Once the obelisk arrived in England there was more trouble – a row immediately started about where it should be put up.

The forecourt of the British Museum was suggested initially; then Kensington Gardens, followed by Greenwich Park, but a site in Parliament Square near the House of Commons was finally decided on. To convince the doubters – of whom there were many – a wooden replica was first built and erected in the square so that Londoners' reaction could be judged. Then disaster struck – the underground railway company whose line ran under the square was convinced that the obelisk would crash through into their tunnel. This argument was seen as compelling and Parliament Square was rejected. After lengthy further debate the obelisk was moved to its present position by the Thames – appropriate enough, given that it was first built to stand by the edge of the Nile and it now stands, as it has for over a century, on the banks of another great river.

If its journey to England was eccentric the pillar's final placing was even more so. The ancient tradition of burying a child's shoe or a coin beneath a new building for good luck was here taken to ridiculous lengths. Among the objects buried beneath the obelisk – and they are still there – are: a model of the hydraulic equipment used to raise the obelisk; a two-foot rule; a child's feeding bottle and some toys; a tin of hairpins, some tobacco, a portrait of Queen Victoria, a map of London and a collection of newspapers; a set of coins, several empty jars; copies of the Bible; a translation of the hieroglyphics on the stone; a copy of *Whitaker's Almanack*; a line of rope and some photographs of famous beauties of the day.

The obelisk is a great survivor, however. Having come through the ravages of more than three thousand years it still bears the marks of bomb damage from the Second World War, and Londoners who grew fond of this oddity in their midst soon came up with a rhyme about it that is somehow both affectionate and dismissive:

This monument as some supposes
Was put up in the time of Moses
It passed in time to the Greeks and Turks
But was put up here by the Board of Works.

PAYING FOR LAND WITH NAILS

1881

The Law Courts in the Strand were built after a competition to find a suitable design. The architect, G. E. Street (1824–1881), won with the Gothic Revival building we see today but the process of implementing the design was dogged by delays caused by some very bizarre architectural requests.

At the outset Street stipulated that standard bricks would be no good for his building, so more than 30 million odd-sized bricks had to be produced at huge cost. The next difficulty was that bricklayers from Germany had to be brought over to complete the work as all London's bricklayers boycotted the work after a row. Street became so concerned about progress on the building that his health declined and he died before the last brick was laid.

But the strangest thing about the law courts is that each year, in a ceremony dating back to the early twelfth century, officials from the Corporation of London come here to pay rent for a piece of ground in Shropshire, owned by the Crown but leased by the Corporation.

The rent is paid in kind: it consists of a billhook and a scythe. Another small patch of ground on Chancery Lane and also owned by the Crown is paid for annually at the law courts in a slightly different way. For this second patch of ground the Corporation of London hands over the princely sum of six horse shoes and sixty nails!

ROYAL SCULPTOR WORKS FROM GAOL

1886

There are two bizarre tales about the statue of Queen Anne that stands in front of the entrance to St Paul's Cathedral. It's not the original statue that was completed in 1712 because by the end of the nineteenth century the original was so worn by time, pigeon droppings, coal smog and vandalism that the authorities decided to commission a new statue.

Public sculpture was far more in demand in Victorian England than it is now and many artists whose names mean nothing today were virtually household names a century and more ago.

When a new statue of Queen Anne was needed the City approached the celebrated sculptor Richard Claude Belt. He promised to complete the work in the year it was commissioned – 1886 – but then it all went disastrously wrong. Like many artists Belt was talented but a bit of a reprobate. He was constantly running up debts and getting into scrapes, and about the time he accepted the commission for the new statue of Queen Anne he got into a particularly bad scrape and was imprisoned for fraud. He'd spent the first part of the money advanced for the statue. The city authorities had no intention of throwing that money away by commissioning another artist to start all over again but they couldn't just get Belt released. The answer was to get special permission to deliver stone and tools to Belt's cell!

And that's exactly what happened, with the result that we can confidently say that the St Paul's statue of Queen Anne is the only public work of art completed by a convicted prisoner while he was actually in prison.

Belt's statue was threatened with demolition a few years later when Queen Victoria celebrated her Diamond Jubilee in 1897. The authorities thought that Anne should be removed to make it easier for the royal coach to sweep up to the front of St Paul's so they went ahead with plans to at least move if not simply do away with Belt's statue, but when the Queen heard of the plan she was furious. She is reported to have said: 'If you remove the statue of Queen Anne for me, who is to say that a statue of me will not be removed to accommodate some future monarch after I am dead?' She was no doubt horrified at the thought that the Prince of Wales, the son she loathed and blamed for her husband's death, would become king and then have his revenge on her by getting rid of the dozens of public statues of her that had gone up all over the country during her long reign.

VIOLINIST HIT BY FISH

1890

It's now quite common in London to see geese flying overhead or swans; even, occasionally, a rarity such as a cormorant. Along the Thames right into the heart of the city herons now stalk the shallows and various wildlife bodies tell us that owls roost in Parliament Square while kestrels hover above the Commercial Road.

In the nineteenth century things were very different, as pollution caused by millions of coal fires – not to mention heavy industry – meant there was far less wildlife than today.

But having said that, London's bigger parks have always provided a haven for wildlife, which is why reports of ducks wandering across Kensington High Street with their ducklings coming along behind were always quite common.

Far less common was the bizarre wildlife encounter in Kensington reported in a Victorian newspaper.

Miss Charlotte Wadham, a young and attractive violinist, was walking home one autumn evening after what the delightfully old-fashioned newspaper reporter described as 'a musical engagement involving the celebrated Mr Bach'. She was halfway up Kensington Church Street when she was struck by what she later described to the newspaper as 'a terrific blow to the side of the head'. In fact the bump was so hard that she was knocked unconscious for a few moments.

One of the witnesses who helped the injured woman into a local house where brandy was administered (much, apparently, to the delight of Miss Wadham) described an extraordinary circumstance that almost certainly accounted for the knockout blow. When the witness had run up to the prostrate Miss Wadham he spotted a large fish lying on the pavement nearby. Being a fisherman he knew that this was not the sort of fish one buys at a fishmonger. It was in fact a roach, a common British freshwater fish, but completely inedible. The witness told the newspaper that at first he could not understand how the fish came to be lying in the street, but in helping the injured woman to her feet he noticed something very odd indeed. The woman's head and the shoulder of her coat were dusted here and there with fish scales. The scales were without question from the dead roach found at the scene.

When the newspaper reporter compiled his report on the incident he quoted a professor of zoology who stated that Miss Wadham was almost certainly felled by a roach dropped by a passing bird, possibly a heron or cormorant.

Miss Wadham's violin, much to her relief, was unharmed.

A RIVER FLYING THROUGH THE AIR

1895

Sloane Square Station now finds itself in one of London's smartest districts. It lies at one end of what was London's first bus route – buses ran from Sloane Square up Sloane Street to Knightsbridge and back again a distance of less than a mile – but the tube station is nothing out of the ordinary. Built at the end of the nineteenth century as part of the District line, it has always served the wealthy residents of Eaton Square and Belgravia. Like so many pioneering railway builders, the men behind the District line were used to overcoming geological and political difficulties, but they were almost stumped by the difficulties surrounding the building of Sloane Square Station.

When the engineers started work they discovered that a river ran across the path of their proposed railway.

The long-hidden River Westbourne rises to the northwest of Hyde Park (hence Westbourne Terrace) and originally flowed through Hyde Park, enabling eighteenth-century engineers to build the Serpentine. But where the water flows out of the Knightsbridge end of the Serpentine it once continued down towards Sloane Square and on to the Thames.

The railway engineers who built Sloane Square Station were temporarily baffled. Eventually they came up with the solution that still makes Sloane Square one of the strangest stations on the whole underground network.

The engineers built a huge round pipe more than five feet in diameter to carry the River Westbourne over the platforms and railway lines –

anyone who gets off at the station today need only look up to see the massive pipe still in position and the river still runs through it.

Intriguingly it is believed that there may even be a few fish still swimming in the pipe – descendants of the roach, perch and gudgeon that once gathered in the shallows when this was a clean sparkling stream running through open country.

COWS IN THE PARK

1905

Despite the best efforts of developers, London's parks have survived the centuries pretty well. Occasionally roads have sliced through some of them – Park Lane, for example, really was a lane before being turned into a six-lane highway for no good reason. The oldest and most interesting of the parks – St James's – was originally established as a hunting ground so kings and courtiers could hunt deer from the nearby palaces of St James and Westminster.

The point of the hunting grounds was not that they should be big enough to give the deer a sporting chance, but that they should be small enough to guarantee a kill. One of the strangest stories associated with St James's has nothing to do with hunting or indeed with royalty. It concerns the small café that still stands near the lake.

The story begins in 1905 when London's planners decided to build the grand semi-circular Admiralty Arch at the Trafalgar Square end of The Mall. The arch was designed to take up only a small area of what had been open space, but there was a problem. Two elderly women had walked to this corner every day for as long as anyone could remember accompanied by three cows. Having arrived at the edge of the park they tethered their cows and set up stall – for a penny a glass passers-by could enjoy a drink of milk, fresh and still warm from the cow. It was a treat much enjoyed by Londoners and visitors alike and the two women made a very good living. But their place of business was in the way of the new arch and the authorities were not going to let them stand in the way of progress.

They were told to remove themselves forthwith, but word leaked to the press and the public rebelled *en masse* – questions were raised in the House of Commons and the Lords and articles by the great and the good appeared in newspapers saying that it was an outrage to remove one of the most delightful traditions associated with the park. But what clinched it for the two elderly dairymaids was that Edward VII remembered drinking at the ladies' corner and he too thought it was an outrage that they should disappear.

The difficulty was that though the ladies claimed an ancient right to sell milk in the park they had no paperwork to prove it. When questioned by a Commons Committee they insisted their families had sold milk in this corner of the park since the mid-seventeenth century. Researchers got to work and uncovered a long history of milk selling in St James's Park. References in obscure documents dating back centuries did indeed make occasional reference to the sale of milk. It was becoming increasingly difficult to justify the removal of the two milkmaids and their cows.

At last the planners relented and the ladies were allowed to stay but they were told they would have to move away from The Mall and closer to the lake. They were also told that the right to sell milk would die with them. In the end this did not happen, however. The last of the two women died in about 1920 but the sale of refreshments did not die with them. The right to sell refreshments in the park seems to have become a right defined simply by long use and the present kiosk, situated where the two women and their cows once plied their trade, exists under that ancient right.

HIDDEN FIGURES ON THE BRIDGE

1906

The modernist movement in architecture seems largely to have consisted of a move to ban all forms of decoration from buildings. For the man on the Clapham omnibus, of course, this meant that the built environment that was once designed to delight and entertain both passers-by and those who lived or worked in a particular building suddenly came to look increasingly dull and utilitarian. It is no accident that critics of modernist architecture see it as a close ally of fascism – cold cruel lines, brutal in their conception and execution came to epitomise the most famous architecture of the 1930s onwards and most famously in the work of Le Corbusier and his followers.

The last great flowering of architecture that could be witty and decorative, playful even, came at the end of the much maligned Victorian era. We tend to think of the Victorians as lacking in grace and humour – an entirely false idea. Their builders and architects loved to embellish and decorate even in areas of a building that would only rarely be seen – much as the builders of medieval churches would encourage their carpenters to carve the underside of pews, the Victorians encouraged a riot of decorative stone, wood and brickwork.

One of the most unusual structures in London came about as a result of just this kind of impulse – in 1906 the present Vauxhall Bridge was finally completed. Like all Victorian and earlier bridges across the

Thames it is enlivened with decorative detail, but what strange impulse persuaded the designers to add eight sculptures that can only be seen with great difficulty?

On the downstream side of the bridge the figures represent science, local government, education and the fine arts; on the upstream side they represent agriculture, sculpture, pottery and engineering.

Among these extraordinary sculptures is a perfect miniature version of St Paul's held in an outstretched hand!

Little St Paul's on the Water, as it has long been affectionately known among watermen, is very difficult to see from the bridge itself – you have to lean over the parapet, but it is worth it!

ONE-LEGGED ESCALATOR TESTER

1910

London's underground railway system is the oldest in the world and many of the tunnels we travel through today are relatively unchanged from when they were first built late in the nineteenth or early in the twentieth century.

When the Piccadilly line opened in 1906 it was the longest underground line in the world, covering more than ten miles. It was later extended to thirty-two and then finally covered more than forty miles, but even at ten miles it was one of the wonders of the world – it was also rather terrifying for passengers unused to travelling below ground.

But hardly had the public got used to this remarkable long-distance underground railway than the company that ran the trains introduced something even more remarkable.

When London's first railway escalator began operating at Earl's Court Station on the Piccadilly line in 1910 the passengers, to a man, were too terrified to use it. The railway company was aghast – they'd paid huge sums to have the revolutionary equipment fitted but it was all wasted if no one would dare use it. Then a bright spark had an idea – why not employ someone to use the escalator throughout the day to give the public confidence? The idea was accepted and Bumper Harris, a man with a wooden leg, was thereafter employed for a number of years to go up and down the escalator all day. Soon the public began to realise that if a man with one leg could use this remarkable new transportation system safely there was no reason why they shouldn't be able to.

Of course Bumper, about whom almost nothing else is known, did his job too well – the public soon thought nothing of using the new moving staircase and he was out of a job.

THE STATUE THAT ISN'T THERE

1912

When Peter Llewellyn Davies, a successful publisher, killed himself in 1960 by throwing himself under a train at Sloane Square, the newspaper headlines were all variations on a theme and that theme was Peter Pan.

Llewellyn Davies, like his four brothers, had been the inspiration for what is one of the most famous characters in children's fiction.

Peter Pan came into existence almost by accident when author J.M. Barrie (1860–1937) met the Llewellyn Davies boys in Kensington Gardens in 1900. He befriended their mother and father and when both died of cancer, Barrie virtually took over the boys' upbringing. He showered them with gifts and paid for their education. The games they played together in Kensington Gardens inspired the story of the boy who never grew up.

Years later the only surviving brother, Nico, told an interviewer that Barrie's motives were not sexual. But there is no doubt that Barrie was an unhappy man who wished to live vicariously, as it were, through the boys he idolised. Certainly his own marriage was a disaster and there were rumours that it was never consummated, for Barrie seems to have loved the idea of being in love – particularly with young actresses – rather than the reality of it.

When *Peter Pan* was first performed in London in 1904 it made Barrie famous – and very rich. In 1912 he conceived the idea of a statue of Peter Pan in the park where he had first played with the Llewellyn Davies boys, but this proved difficult and complex. Statues in the royal parks are permitted only following agreement by Royal Commission or, at the least, a parliamentary committee. But Barrie was world famous by now and not an easy man to refuse. After making enquiries he received an extremely odd reply to his request to erect the statue. He was told that he would not receive permission, but at the same time there would be no objection. On that basis Barrie assumed he could go ahead so he commissioned Sir George Frampton (1860–1928) to make the statue we see today.

Barrie himself unveiled the new statue at midnight and on his own – he liked the idea that children would see it the next morning and assume it had simply appeared as if by magic.

Initially the statue was hated (though not by children) but by 1921 it was the most popular statue in London, a position it almost certainly retains to this day.

But the lives of the boys who inspired the story and the statue were curiously unhappy – despite material wealth and expensive private educations provided by the ever generous Barrie, they seem to have been deeply troubled. Michael Llewellyn Davies, Barrie's favourite of the five brothers, drowned with a close friend during his last year at Oxford. There were rumours that it was a suicide pact and it is certainly true that Michael drowned at a spot on the river where only a good swimmer should have been – Michael could not swim at all. George was killed in action during the First World War and Peter, as we have seen, committed suicide. In Peter's case the connection with Barrie and the story of Peter Pan was almost certainly central to his decision to end his life.

In 1952 he had burned more than two thousand letters between his brother Michael and Barrie – he called the collection of letters 'The Morgue' and told friends that he absolutely loathed the connection with Barrie. It is odd that something that has brought so much pleasure to countless thousands of children across the world should have brought only sorrow to the five children who inspired it. Curious too that their memorial, the statue of Peter Pan, is a statue that, officially at least, isn't even there.

J.M. Barrie himself unveiled the new statue at midnight and on his own – he liked the idea that children would see it the next morning and assume it had simply appeared as if by magic.

THE PALACE THAT FACES
THE WRONG WAY

1912

Buckingham Palace is known throughout the world as the London home of the royal family, but it has a curious and less well-known history. The present building is the fourth on the site and it started life as a small, rather unpretentious house lived in by the Duke of Buckingham.

Built at the end of the seventeenth century, the original house bore no resemblance to the present building. Buckingham sold it in 1761 to George III, who wanted it for his wife Charlotte. Some fourteen of George's fifteen children were born in the house.

William Chambers (1723–1796) was brought in to partly rebuild and remodel the house in 1762 and it was left alone then until the 1820s when John Nash (1752–1835) doubled the size of the main block and refaced the house with Bath stone. He demolished a couple of wings and had Marble Arch made as a triumphal entrance to a new courtyard – Marble Arch was then discovered to be too narrow for the royal coach.

One would have thought that the designers would have measured a coach or two before going ahead – they didn't because they wanted the arch to be an exact copy of the Roman Triumphal Arch of Constantine. George IV and his architect John Nash wanted to reflect the dignity of ancient Rome, but in their obsession with ancient precedent they forgot modern practicality. The width of the arch itself is perfect for a Roman chariot but far too narrow for a Georgian coach. The embarrassing arch was moved in 1851 to an isolated spot at the end of the Edgware Road and there it has stayed ever since. And still to this day only royal coaches are allowed to go through the arch – except, of course, they don't fit so it remains unused.

But back to Buckingham House. After spending more than half a million pounds of taxpayers' money (the budget was £150,000) on it George IV died in 1830 having never actually lived in the house. His 'improvements' were still unfinished. The new king, William IV, spent more money on the house.

It's easy to forget that before Queen Victoria and the growth in which they took part of newspapers, which brought a sense of the monarch as a public figure, the royal family did not care what the general public thought of them. They lived private lives and the grand public ceremonies were only ever seen by other important people. If a king spent too much money on a project no one would dare criticise them anyway, although Parliament might grumble.

But as the monarchy realised that its public role was developing and that it had to show its face to the world, a decision was taken to turn Buckingham Palace around so that instead of facing into its private park it would face down The Mall in a decidedly public manner. This is why what we think of as the front of the palace is actually the back – the 'real' front faces the private park as it has always done.

It was Victoria who had the east front added in the 1840s by Edward Blore (1787–1879). For the first time the house faced down The Mall.

But the endless tampering with the house didn't end there – Blore's French stone was considered too soft so it was replaced a few decades later by the architect Sir Aston Webb (1849–1930) using the rather harsh Portland stone we see today.

A CARRIAGE PULLED BY ZEBRAS

1920

Aristocrats traditionally have the time and the money to indulge the most obscure, eccentric tastes. And the combination of money and eccentricity has always produced Londoners of exceptional lunacy.

Take Walter Rothschild (1868–1937), for example. Decidedly but brilliantly eccentric, he hated speaking to people, was blackmailed out of a fortune by his mistress and trained three zebras to pull his carriage along Pall Mall. Unfitted for the normal routes into public life that Rothschild elder sons tended to take, he set up a natural history museum that eventually grew into the biggest private museum in the world.

Throughout his life he was prepared to pay almost anything for a rare or unusual specimen, and by 1920, after working in virtual seclusion for years for eighteen hours a day, he had amassed some two thousand complete mounted animals, two hundred animal heads, three hundred sets of antlers, three thousand stuffed birds, seven hundred reptiles, one thousand stuffed fish, three hundred thousand bird skins and two hundred thousand birds' eggs. He was a brilliant if utterly obsessive zoological classifier – his enthusiasm and dedication was eventually rewarded when a subspecies of giraffe was named after him.

The stories of his madcap adventures in London are legion. Among the best is the story of his motorcar outing in Hyde Park. He was hurtling through the park and had reached the bridge over the Serpentine when he spotted a chauffeur standing outside a stationary car with a folded rug over his arm. Rothschild immediately shouted at his own driver to stop. He leaped from the car, explaining that the rug in the other chauffeur's arms was made from the pelts of extremely rare tree kangaroos. Having waited till the owner of the rug arrived he refused to leave until the rug had been sold to him – the owner of the rug was shrewd enough to demand an absurdly high price but Rothschild would have paid almost anything.

ANCIENT HALL GOES TO CHELSEA

1925

London is constantly changing and in various periods the pace of that change may increase or decrease, but in essence it never stops, which is why buildings built before 1700 are so rare.

Perhaps the most interesting, bizarre and least-known early building is Crosby Hall, which was built near Bishopsgate in the City of London by Sir John Crosby, a wealthy wool merchant. The house was completed between 1466 and 1475 and though it is no longer in Bishopsgate it survives because of the enthusiasm of a group of preservationists in the 1920s.

Crosby Hall now stands in Chelsea near the site of Sir Thomas More's (1478–1535) former home. The hall is largely complete – it has its original roof and oriel window and is the only remaining tangible evidence of how the wealthy built in fifteenth-century London.

It was moved stone by stone in 1925, but is substantially unaltered and the last example left of a medieval London merchant's house. The casual visitor may think as he passes the house on the north bank of the Thames near Cheyne Walk that it is a piece of fake Gothic architecture but he'd be mistaken – this is the real thing.

THE WORLD'S MOST FAMOUS PARROT

1926

Archaeology is not just about discovering how the great lived or worshipped. It's also about how the poor lived – but as the poor tend to have less they have tended to leave fewer artifacts in the archaeological record. Which is why an occasional commonplace survival from an earlier era deserves the attention it often gets. One such survival is the Cheshire Cheese public house just off London's Fleet Street.

In 1666 the Great Fire of London destroyed Old St Paul's, crept down Ludgate Hill towards the River Fleet and even destroyed a number of houses on the west of the river in what is today Fleet Street. But a few houses did escape the flames only to be destroyed – for example – when the hideous modern buildings of King's College were built.

Fleet Street was always famously bordered by a mass of tangled courts and alleyways typical of a crowded city that had grown slowly over many centuries.

Most of these courts and alleys are now built over or lined with dull office buildings but in Wine Office Court there is a most surprising survivor – a late seventeenth-century pub that looks exactly inside as it would have looked when it was first built. What's more, the interior is not a re-creation – the tables in the public bar, the fireplace, the décor and the pictures on the wall have all been here for at least two hundred years.

The fame of the Cheshire Cheese spread far and wide and from the 1850s it was on the itinerary of most visitors to London.

If we compare the interior of the Cheshire Cheese to prints and drawings of early London coffee houses we realise that the Cheese is the last of these long-vanished and once hugely popular features of London life.

The fame of the Cheshire Cheese spread far and wide and from the 1850s it was on the itinerary of most visitors to London.

And by 1900 the pub had a resident who was to become almost as famous as the Cheese itself – this was Polly the Eccentric Parrot. Polly was known across the world for her bizarre antics and for her intelligence and abilities as a mimic. Famously garrulous and rude about visitors she didn't like, Polly celebrated the end of the First World War in 1918 in her own way. She imitated the noise of champagne corks popping an estimated four hundred times and then fell off her perch suffering from exhaustion.

When she died in 1926 she was estimated to be over forty and her antics over the years she spent at the Cheshire Cheese earned her an accolade unique in the animal kingdom – her obituary appeared in more than two hundred newspapers worldwide.

Polly lived at the Cheese during its most famous days but the list of celebrities who drank here is extraordinary: mostly literary figures are associated with the pub – Dr Johnson, who lived just two minutes' walk away in Gough Square, is reported to have come here every night for years along with his friend and biographer James Boswell (1740–1795); Dickens sat through many long evenings in the corner by the door in the room opposite the public bar; in the eighteenth century the actor and impresario David Garrick (1717–1779) came here with his friends the painter Sir Joshua Reynolds (1723–1792) and Edward Gibbon (1737–1794), author of *The Decline and Fall of the Roman Empire*; in the nineteenth century as well as Dickens, Wilkie Collins (1824–1889) was a regular together with Tennyson (1809–1892) and Carlyle (1795–1881); by the twentieth century everyone from Theodore Roosevelt (1858–1919) to Mark Twain (1835–1910) and Conan Doyle (1859–1930) came.

Above the fireplace in the public bar is a fascinating portrait dating from 1829, darkened by the smoke from countless candles and coal fires, of the waiter William Simpson. Apart from the fact that paintings of servants are rare the picture is interesting because the very table on which Simpson leans in his portrait is still in the bar nearby.

In the nineteenth century, the Cheese had one other claim to eccentricity: its landlord made some of the biggest pies in London. Filled with beef, oysters and lark each pie weighed between fifty and eighty pounds! Each was big enough to feed about 100 people and among those who ceremonially dished up the first serving were Sir Arthur Conan Doyle and future Prime Minister Stanley Baldwin (1867–1947).

A STATUE WITH ITS OWN INCOME

1929

St Dunstan's Church in Fleet Street is one of London's oddest churches. For a start it is octagonal in shape – the result of an oddly shaped site – and for many years it provided a home to a number of strange Christian sects: the Coptic Ethiopian Church, the Assyrian Church, the Romanian Orthodox Church and the Old Catholic Church of Utrecht.

Now hemmed in on all sides by later rebuilding, the churchyard was once a thriving place of business. Anyone who has a collection of seventeenth- and eighteenth-century books will see on the title page again and again the address 'Published at St Dunstan's in the West' followed by the date, for St Dunstan's, like St Paul's less than a mile away, was once a great centre of book publishing.

The most reprinted book after the Bible was first printed here – Izaak Walton's *The Compleat Angler* (far more a book about the contemplative life than about fishing) was sold here by Walton himself, who lived here and was St Dunstan's churchwarden for many years.

But the strangest feature of St Dunstan's is the statue of Elizabeth I that stands just in front of the church. Carved in the 1580s while the Queen was still alive it stood for many years on Ludgate where the Queen would regularly have seen it on her progresses from Westminster to the City and back. When Ludgate was demolished at the end of the eighteenth century the statue was brought to St Dunstan's.

The statue has been here ever since and it is the only statue in London (probably the only statue in the world) that has its own income.

In 1929 the philanthropist Lady Millicent Fawcett, concerned that the statue should be properly looked after, left enough money in trust for it to be cleaned and repaired in perpetuity.

FISHING FROM THE ROOF OF THE SAVOY

1930

The Savoy Hotel and surrounding area is rich in history, much of it bizarre in the extreme, but there are also odd endearing tales that attach themselves to the modern hotel and the ancient palace that once stood on the Thameside site.

One of the best of these tales concerns two guests staying at the hotel back in the 1930s.

Like the English, Americans are obsessed with fishing with rod and line and to the enthusiast half the pleasure of fishing is arguing about flies and lines and the various techniques for casting them.

Two Americans staying at the Savoy in London were particularly keen on fishing and over dinner one evening they had an argument over whether or not it would be possible to cast a fly, using a salmon rod, from the roof of their hotel over the gardens and the busy Embankment and into the Thames.

They were so determined to settle the dispute that they went along to Hardy Brothers, the tackle-makers in Pall Mall, and asked them to decide if such a thing was possible. Hardy Brothers approached the angler and author Esmond Drury who agreed to attempt the feat on condition that he was tied securely to a chimney on the hotel roof.

Early one Sunday morning, and with the help of a policeman who stopped all the traffic on the Embankment, he proved that it was indeed possible to cast a fly into the Thames from the roof of the Savoy.

But the Savoy has always been a place that generates eccentricities. Take the short street at the front where taxis pull up to pick up hotel guests – this short stretch of roadway is the only place in the country where traffic is allowed to drive on the wrong side of the road. No one knows why this is but cars and taxis here must drive on the right.

The Savoy stands on the site of the old medieval Savoy Palace built by Henry III's friend Count Peter of Savoy in 1264. The courtyard at the front of the present hotel is said to follow the lines of the original medieval courtyard palace. The present building, completed in 1889, was commissioned and paid for by Richard D'Oyly Carte (1844–1901) using the vast sums he made putting on Gilbert and Sullivan operas. The famous Peach Melba was invented here (in honour of the great opera diva Nellie Melba), as was the dry martini. And legend has it that if thirteen guests find themselves about to sit down to supper the hotel will provide a fourteenth guest (a black cat) to avoid the bad luck inherent in the number 13.

And there is a long tradition at the hotel that if the guest is important enough they will put up with almost anything – one guest turned up with her pet crocodile, others have appeared with monkeys; marmosets and parrots are virtually commonplace. Two final strange tales about the Savoy: an American guest once took pot shots with his 12-bore shotgun from the roof at geese flying towards Green Park, and the great violinist Jascha Heifetz once had bagpipe lessons on the roof.

A little further west along the Strand from the Savoy is a short street that once ran down to the river. Savoy Street will take you to the Savoy Chapel, parts of which certainly date back to the original foundation, which is contemporaneous with Count Peter's twelfth-century palace. Most of the present building is relatively recent but it was once the cause of a bizarre legal suit. Having reverted to the Crown following the death of Peter of Savoy (1203–1268) the chapel was given to the Duke of Lancaster – who also happened to be the king. This meant the chapel was owned both by the king and by the Duke of Lancaster, but as they were one and the same person confusion reigned. The difficulty was only eliminated in the early eighteenth century when the king sued the Duke (i.e. he sued himself) to establish who had the right to the chapel and the land on which it was built. Not surprisingly the king won.

THE BUILDING THAT'S REALLY AN ADVERTISEMENT

1930

In the early part of the twentieth century, London was still a rather strait-laced place where advertising was considered rather vulgar – to the extent that it was banned on the sides of buildings. Partly this was an attempt to tidy up after the chaos of earlier centuries when shopkeepers and tradesmen put signs outside their shops and then tried to outdo each other by gradually making their signs bigger or attaching them to long poles until narrow streets would be dark all day because of the shadows cast by countless signs.

The first buses were also covered in ads, which then began to creep up the sides of buildings until the authorities called a halt. Tall buildings began to appear and though they would have provided magnificent sites for advertisements the authorities were horrified at the prospect. But one or two advertisers were determined to get round the ban and in at least one strange instance they got away with it.

On the south bank near Blackfriars Bridge a tower was built above a warehouse. The tower still survives and is now home to a very fashionable restaurant which offers diners a magnificent view from their tables along the river. At the top of the tower and visible from miles away there is an advertisement for the famous Oxo beef cube. The ad has been here since the building was first put up and it escaped the ban to which all such similar ads would have been subject. It did it by incorporating the advertisement – the letters OXO – into the very structure of the building. What look like three big letters are in fact three gigantic windows filled with red glass.

COWS IN THE STRAND

1930

Until relatively recently all London's food supplies had to be brought fresh to the capital – in the days before refrigeration there was no alternative, which explains why live animals were driven to Smithfield well into the twentieth century and milk was sold in various parks around London straight from the cow. Until 1900 you might often have seen a flock of geese marching towards London, each bird wearing a pair of tar boots (their feet were dipped in tar to prevent the long walk causing bleeding and pain).

But London was also a curiously unregulated place and the authorities were often more astonished than anyone to discover that odd trades and crafts were still being carried on long after everyone had assumed they were extinct.

Down by the river about halfway between Waterloo and Charing Cross Bridges was the world's first block of flats. Adelphi Terrace, completed in 1768, was built by the Adam brothers and was split into apartments – to the utter astonishment of Londoners who had never seen anything like it before.

Sadly little remains of this marvellous scheme and the superb buildings that once stood here. Most were demolished in the 1930s (one part survives in nearby Adam Street) but it was discovered as demolition got under way that an elderly woman was still living in the building along with half a dozen cows whose milk she sold in the Strand!

Dozens of other curious tales attach to this most historic and relatively little-altered part of London – J. M. Barrie of *Peter Pan* fame and George Bernard Shaw, for example, lived opposite each other for a while in Robert Street and when they wanted a break from writing they would throw biscuits or cherry stones at each other's windows to attract attention.

Another story tells how the Adam brothers wanted the building work on the Adelphi carried out as cheaply as possible so they brought workers down from Scotland. The workers quickly found out how much less than the going rate they were being paid and went on strike, so the brothers set off for Ireland where they employed Irish labourers, but only those who could speak no English! But the canny Irish, though they spoke only Gaelic, were not so easily fooled. Within days of their starting work in London they knew they were being swindled – the Adam brothers forgot that many of the workers would have had relatives in London and they quickly discovered what they should have been paid. In the face of another threat of strike action the Adam brothers quietly gave in and paid up.

TOP-SECRET GRASS-CUTTING SERVICE

1940

In its present triumphal form The Mall was laid out in the nineteenth century to emulate the triumphal routes of various other capitals – for example, Paris and Rome. It joins Trafalgar Square to Buckingham Palace, passing Horse Guards Parade on the way. The Mall is a familiar thoroughfare, but just where it passes Horse Guards Parade there is a very odd building that most people completely fail to notice.

Built from dark-red bricks and almost always covered in ivy, the building has a fortress feel about it – there is no decorative brickwork and not a ground-floor window in sight.

The building was made to protect the admiralty communications centre from bombs during the Second World War and almost nothing about it appears in any guide book about London.

When it was first put up the press was forbidden to mention it and everything possible was done to make sure it was undetectable, particularly from the air, and impregnable. The walls are incredibly thick and there is no doubt that it would withstand a conventional bomb or two, but just to be on the safe side the military decided that the best way to hide the building from the air would be to plant grass on top of it.

However, this led to one extremely eccentric proceeding which continues to this day – every morning in summer an employee carrying his top-secret pass presents himself to the officials within the building and is allowed to enter. He carries with him a lawn mower – this has to be carried out through an upstairs window onto a set of steps that lead to the roof. He mows the grass, carries his mower back downstairs across the office floor and out of the building.

HOW ST PAUL'S HAD A MIRACULOUS ESCAPE

1940

The Blitz on London – the word is from the German *Blitzkrieg* meaning lightning war – destroyed almost as much of the beautiful ancient City as the planners and developers of the 1950s and 1960s.

Despite its great size and the fact that, from the air, St Paul's Cathedral was an easy target, London's greatest church was not destroyed during the Blitz – in fact it was scarcely touched at all, despite the rain of bombs that fell in the area month after month. The fact of St Paul's survival is well known, but it is only when we look in detail at the number and size of bombs that fell that we realise quite what a miraculous escape the church had.

The bombing began in September 1940. Before that date Hitler had concentrated his attacks on British RAF fields and more obviously military targets, but the indiscriminate bombing of London that began in September showed that Hitler would stop at nothing to win the war. His actions over London and later Coventry were to lead ultimately to the fire bombing of Dresden and other horrors.

For 57 nights London was bombed every night and frequently also during the day. Between September 1940 and May 1941 almost nineteen thousand tonnes of high explosive rained down on the capital. Largely residential areas such as Southwark and Holborn were very badly damaged.

Through the early weeks of the Blitz the historic area of smaller houses and offices that were in many cases just yards from St Paul's in a warren of tiny ancient streets were completely flattened by direct hits. The whole of the historic booksellers area of Paternoster Row vanished forever, but right in the midst of this firestorm St Paul's remained unscathed for reasons that really cannot be adequately explained – expert fire watching certainly helped and the cathedral was also just very lucky. Disaster came very close indeed when on 12 September a bomb fell right next to the southwest tower but failed to explode. It buried itself deep underground and hard up against the church foundations – only the skill and bravery of the firefighters who spent three days extricating the bomb prevented disaster. When the bomb was finally removed it was still live. It was placed on the back of a truck and carried at a snail's pace to Hackney Marshes where it was detonated – the resulting crater measured more than one hundred feet across.

A GIFT TO LONDON – A GERMAN LAMPPOST

1963

The practice of town twinning is bizarre – for many it simply provides an excuse for local officials to enjoy all-expenses-paid trips to foreign countries; for those who enjoy such trips, twinning represents (perhaps) a hand of friendship extended across the seas to nations with whom we are already friendly.

Perhaps the odd, slightly dubious, nature of twinning explains one of the strangest gifts ever given by one nation to another.

Anyone who walks along the north side of the Thames above Hammersmith Bridge will see the old inns and boathouses that have characterised the area for centuries, but tucked away against the wall of an old house the eagle-eyed may spot something very different – a worn rectangular metal plaque. The plaque records that in 1963 Herr Willy Brandt (1913–1992), later the German Chancellor, gave the good citizens of Hammersmith a lamppost. The gift was to mark the twinning of Hammersmith with the borough of Neukölln in Berlin.

The plaque solemnly declares that 'The lamp above this plaque was formerly used to light a street in West Berlin. It was presented by Herr Willy Brandt, the Mayor of West Berlin, to councillor Stanley Atkins as a token of friendship.'

Whether the lamp has some symbolic significance – perhaps to shed light on the relationship or to illuminate the dark past of European history is anyone's guess. One wonders what Hammersmith gave West Berlin – perhaps a manhole cover or a stretch of municipal railing!

CAMPAIGNING AGAINST PEANUTS AND SITTING

1965

Strange stories and strange characters are not entirely a feature of London's more distant past. Anyone over fifty who knows London well will remember a very odd character who haunted Oxford Street and Regent Street for several decades.

Stanley Green died at the age of seventy-eight in 1992, having spent nearly thirty years parading the West End carrying a placard warning mostly against the dangers of protein.

Over the years he sold tens of thousands of hand-printed leaflets (at 12p each) explaining why lustful feelings were induced by 'fish, birds, meat, cheese, egg, peas, beans, nuts and sitting'. He had worked for many years in a perfectly ordinary job in the civil service before starting his one-man campaign against lust and peanut eating in the early 1960s.

No one really knows why he decided that protein was the root of all the world's evils but once he'd made his decision he never gave up.

'Protein makes passion,' he would say to anyone who would listen. 'If we eat less of it, the world will be a happier place.'

He produced his leaflets on a small press in his tiny flat in north west London; the tenants below often complained about the terrific sounds of thumping and crashing on print day. Until he qualified for a free bus pass he would cycle each day to Oxford Street in his raincoat, cap and wire-rimmed spectacles, and always recalled with pleasure that motorists reading the board on the back of his bicycle would toot their horns and wave. 'I've known coaches pass,' he said, 'and everyone has stood up and cheered me.'

He was occasionally spat at, but he was rarely upset by abuse, explaining that people only attacked him because they thought he was a religious person, which he most clearly was not. He would often concentrate his efforts on cinema queues, using such opening gambits as 'You cannot deceive your groom that you are a virgin on your wedding night.'

CABMAN'S REVENGE

1965

For centuries London's cabmen and porters were vital to the efficient running of the city, but as long as they continued their work nothing much was thought of them. In the eighteenth century this began to change when a porter's rest was put up in Piccadilly – this strange–looking contraption is a broad thick plank of wood set on two cast-iron pillars. The plank would be at chest or even shoulder height for the average man. The reason it was fixed at this height is that it allowed the porters to ease any load off their shoulders and on to the plank, which was almost at the same height, rather than have to lower it to any significant extent. The porter's rest allowed them to slip their load off and on again easily.

Hansom cabs were the great feature of the second half of the nineteenth century (particularly after Poet Laureate Sir John Betjeman's grandfather invented a new lock for their doors) and they grew massively in numbers until the advent of the First World War – after 1918 they rapidly disappeared as motor cabs took over.

But the harsh conditions under which the Victorian hansom-cab drivers had to work – out in all weathers for twelve or more hours a day, seven days a week – came to the attention of a group of philanthropists who started the cabmen's shelter fund in 1874. Their money was used to establish a set of green timber buildings – usually set in the middle of broad thoroughfares – where the cabmen could stop for a cup of tea or lunch or dinner. Many of these cabmen's shelters have now disappeared but thankfully those that remain are now protected. They are always painted green and look rather like large slightly ornate garden sheds with small windows and a pitched roof.

One such cabmen's shelter survives in the Brompton Road near Knightsbridge. Another can be found just off Sloane Street. A third, in Temple Place just north of the Embankment, was the cause of one of the oddest building disputes of the past two centuries.

When in the 1960s a proposal was lodged by developers to knock down four ancient streets running down to Temple Place, officials at the Greater London Council agreed to allow the demolition despite the fact that the hotel planned for the site was designed to house tourists who presumably were coming to London to see the sort of sites their hotel was about to destroy.

The disgraceful demolition plan got the go-ahead and the vast hotel was built but as it neared completion the dozy architects realised that just at the spot they'd planned to put their grand hotel entrance there was a green cabmen's shelter.

With typical corporate stupidity they tried to use their financial might to have the shelter removed by the authorities, but they were told that the shelter had been there since 1880 and it was staying put. Filled with horror that their rich American clients would baulk at the sight of a ramshackle old cab shelter in front of their new hotel, the directors of the building firm had to approach the cabmen cap in hand and ask if they would mind if their shelter were moved a few yards down the street. The cabmen – far more civilised than the corporate bigwigs – agreed provided that the hotel owners paid for the shelter to be moved and made a donation to the cabmen's shelter fund. No doubt the hotel paid as little into the fund as they could, but the shelter was duly – and very carefully – moved a few yards along the road.

'HOW NOT TO GET LOST IN LIBERTY'S'

1970

One of London's most famous shops since it was opened by Arthur Liberty, a Buckinghamshire draper, in 1875, Liberty's was the ultimate in fashion between 1880 and 1920 and it has always been associated with the Arts and Crafts movement. The shop originally sold Japanese fans – Mr Liberty was one of the first to import oriental goods as well as silks and other fabrics in bulk.

Then in 1925, flushed with success, the company, which had by now acquired three adjacent shops, decided to rebuild. The result was the extraordinary mock Tudor building we see today, but this is only visible in Great Marlborough Street. On the side of the store that faces Regent Street, Liberty had to stick to the Portland stone from which the rest of Regent Street is built, but in Great Marlborough Street he could do what he liked. And in the great tradition of craftsmanship and individuality championed by William Morris (1834–1896), the man behind the Arts and Crafts movement, Liberty really let himself go in Great Marlborough Street.

Built around an interior courtyard, Liberty's conceals a remarkable and bizarre secret – it is made almost entirely from the magnificent oak timbers from two dismantled ships, HMS *Hindustan* and HMS *Impregnable*.

Not content with this, the owners of what was and still is one of London's most successful shops employed the best craftsmen – including several brought here specially from Italy – to install stained glass, magnificent staircases and superb carvings. Everything is handmade and unique.

What really ensured the success of Liberty's, however, was not the spectacular building, but the decision made much earlier by Gilbert and Sullivan to use Liberty fabrics for the costumes in their light opera *Patience* (1881).

Perhaps the most delightfully eccentric thing about Liberty's is that its staircases are built in such an odd way that at one time customers were always getting lost. All was resolved when, in the 1970s the then owners published a booklet which was available free to all regular customers entitled 'How Not To Get Lost In Liberty's'!

PENIS FOR SALE AT CHRISTIE'S

1972

When Napoleon Bonaparte died in May 1821 there were fears that rumours would spread about the manner of his death (recent claims include the suggestion that he was poisoned), which may explain why no fewer than seventeen witnesses were invited to observe the autopsy which was carried out the day after he died by the Emperor's own doctor, Francesco Antommarchi.

On the Emperor's own instructions, his heart was removed first. Napoleon had asked that it be sent to his wife Marie-Louise, though the heart apparently vanished before it could be delivered.

The stomach was carefully examined and at the time it was agreed that cancer was the cause of death. Nothing else is recorded as having been removed. However within a few decades it was commonly supposed that Napoleon's penis had been cut off and stored away carefully during the autopsy. Oddly this was not mentioned by any of the seventeen witnesses present at the time of the autopsy. But several commentators have suggested that the body was not guarded at all times during the procedure and while everyone's backs were turned Napoleon's organ could have been quickly snipped off.

Napoleon's friend Vignali, who administered the last rites, was left a large sum of money in Napoleon's will as well as numerous 'personal effects' – these were not specified. Thirty years later Napoleon's manservant claimed that Vignali had indeed removed various parts of Napoleon's body, but this was not corroborated.

By 1916 the material bequeathed to Vignali had been sold *en masse* to a London collector, who some years later sold the collection on to an American. It was at this point that the penis story became more substantial. The description of the collection included the curious phrase mentioning 'the mummified tendon taken from Napoleon's body during the post-mortem'.

By the 1930s A. S. Rosenbach, an American collector, was displaying the 'tendon' in a blue velvet case and describing it as Napoleon's penis. It travelled to France and was later the centrepiece of a grand display at the Museum of French Art in New York.

A newspaper report described the organ as looking 'something like a maltreated strip of buckskin shoelace or shriveled eel'. Reports – largely stemming from Napoleon himself – that he was particularly well endowed seem to be contradicted by the fact that the organ was also described as 'one inch long and resembling a grape'.

The most extraordinary part of the story occurred in London in 1972 when the putative penis was put up for sale – complete with magnificent velvet-lined case – at the London auction house Christie's along with the rest of the Vignali collection. The collection failed to reach its reserve and was withdrawn. A few years later the penis popped up again, this time in Paris and unencumbered by all the other paraphernalia of the collection.

The penis was bought by John Lattimer, a retired professor of urology (appropriately enough) at the University of Columbia, for around $3,000. The penis is still, as it were, in Professor Lattimer's hands.

TEARING UP £80,000

1979

Before he became rich and famous the painter Francis Bacon (1909–92) used to take his friends several times a week to Wheeler's Oyster Bar in Soho. He almost always insisted on paying despite having no regular income at all, which meant that he often had to ask the owner to allow him to run up a tab. Such was Bacon's astonishing charisma that the restaurant owner allowed the bill to reach more than ten thousand pounds before he began to complain. Bacon had become quite well known by this time and the restaurant owner begrudgingly accepted a small Bacon painting as a sort of surety that the bill would eventually be paid. It was paid long before Bacon became a multimillionaire but the restaurateur kept the picture and eventually sold it for more than a quarter of a million pounds. A rare case of justified faith in an artist!

Bacon – a famous and outrageous habitué of Soho bars (most especially The Colony and the French House) – was for decades at the centre of an outrageous clique of artists and writers around whom strange stories swirled like a dangerous mist. Among the most delightful stories is that he once spotted one of his own paintings in a shop in Bond Street and decided he didn't like it. He stepped into the shop, wrote a cheque for something in the region of £80,000, stepped back outside with the carefully wrapped picture under his arm and then smashed it to pieces on the roadway, grinding the canvas underfoot until it was beyond the powers of any restorer to recover it.

ENDLESS SECRET TUNNELS

1980

When journalist Duncan Campbell found an entrance to a shaft in the middle of a traffic island in Bethnal Green in London's East End, he was astonished to discover a large tunnel at the bottom that led away into the distance apparently heading towards central London some half a dozen miles distant.

Campbell went home, collected his folding bike, and some time later returned to the shaft entrance. He carried the bike down the shaft and started pedalling towards central London along a series of extraordinary tunnels.

Over the centuries the curious have regularly come across underground tunnels beneath London's streets – some are ancient, others, as Campbell discovered, more modern. But the oddest thing is that there are almost certainly far more tunnels – many-layered and interconnecting – than we imagine.

Campbell's tunnel started about one hundred feet down and he rode around the tunnels for hours covering in excess of a dozen miles in total, but it was clear to him, as it has been to others, that he had barely scratched the surface of London's extraordinary underground tunnel network.

Beautifully built brick-lined sewers, some dating back to medieval times, certainly exist in the oldest parts of the city and it is still possible to walk along the old bed of the Fleet River, which is now buried beneath Farringdon Street at the bottom of Ludgate Hill. The river –

reduced to little more than a trickle – runs along the bottom of a giant pipe but there is plenty of room to walk.

In Victorian times the vast network of ancient sewers provided a living for hundreds of men and children – intimate knowledge of the tunnel routes was passed from one generation to the next and a team of sewer searchers might travel from the city to the West End and back in a day and always entirely underground, but they had to be careful: a sudden storm in Highgate or Hampstead could lead to flooding – a torrent of water hurtling along the tunnels would sweep the men to their deaths. Experienced sewer men knew the dangers and posted lookouts before they went down as well as trying to restrict their activities to days when the weather was fine. In the thick layers of human fat that lined the tunnels they would often find a rich store of lost gold trinkets and coins.

Those sewers are still there and beneath them, far deeper and almost as deep as London's water table, is a vast array of tunnels that some believe are part of a nuclear network of bunkers centred on Whitehall. There is some evidence for this too. We know, for example, that when the Jubilee line was built planning permission for certain routes was refused but officials would not say why. The same happens when telecommunications tunnels have to be dug – certain areas and depths and routes are always out of bounds because London under London is still the capital's greatest and most complex secret.

LOST LAVATORIES

1985

One of the great tragedies of the past fifty years is the gradual disappearance of London's magnificent public lavatories. Built into the fabric of the environment by nineteenth-century urban planners who were concerned (unlike modern developers) that their buildings should be decorative as well as functional, public lavatories tended to be built at major street junctions and below ground.

But, much as the Victorian pub builder wanted to celebrate his skill in the sumptuousness of gin palaces with their sparkling cut glass, fabulous mirrors and huge ornate ceilings and walls, so the lavatory builders created splendid subterranean palaces of gleaming copper pipework, hugely decorative tiles and basins, and lavatories with delicate flower decoration. Heavy mahogany doors were used for each lavatory cubicle and the overall impression was always one of spacious loftiness, for these were palaces to ease and bodily contentment.

As it cost a penny to use these grand public conveniences the Victorian lavatory also gave us the splendid euphemism that survives to this day: the phrase 'I'm going to spend a penny' being among the politest and most delicate indications that one wishes to use the loo.

The grand Victorian lavatories were gradually taken out of use by penny-pinching local authorities who simply assumed that the growth in cafés and restaurants would fill the gap – if the modern city dweller needs to spend a penny she has to go into an expensive restaurant for a cup of coffee she may well not want simply to use the loo.

But oddly, though many of the old public loos were closed and their entrances sealed over, many still exist complete with all their magnificent pipework below ground, buried like Egyptian tombs and awaiting some enthusiastic future lavatorial archaeologist.

One of the last lavatories to go was the splendid example in Covent Garden just outside the church in the piazza. Here in its dying days in the 1980s you could spend a penny and listen to opera, for the lavatory attendant was a keen opera buff who also decorated the walls with reproductions of some of the National Gallery's most famous pictures. Tourists and Londoners flocked to this eccentric destination, and rightly so, until it was closed by unimaginative local officials.

Odder still than the Covent Garden lavatory was the public loo that once stood in the middle of the road about halfway along High Holborn.

So magnificent were the fittings in this the ultimate public lavatory that they are now in the Victoria and Albert Museum, a testament to the public-spiritedness and architectural pride of our Victorian ancestors.

The brass and mahogany fittings of the Holborn public loo were surmounted by a set of superb cut-glass cisterns. These were spectacular enough to provoke comment in numerous newspapers but the enthusiasm of the public for them knew no bounds when an attendant in the 1930s decided that each cistern would be far more interesting stocked with goldfish. He duly stocked them and the fish lived happily in the sparkling clean water to the delight of patrons for many years – until in fact the Holborn public loo suffered the fate of almost every other public loo in London.

HOW CRIME BECAME ART

1995

In 1962 the future playwright Joe Orton, whose plays *Loot* and *Entertaining Mr Sloane* were later to astonish theatregoers, was arrested along with his lover for defacing library books.

Contrast that with the last year of Orton's extraordinary – and sadly rather short – life. The year 1967 saw the first performance of his play *What the Butler Saw,* the latest in a string of theatrical successes. But Kenneth Halliwell, Orton's lover since 1951, found it difficult to cope with his partner's increasing fame and in a fit of depression killed Orton with a hammer while he slept and then took a massive overdose of sleeping pills.

The newspaper obituaries tended to dwell on what was then described as Orton's 'unnatural relationship' with Halliwell and his outrageous behaviour.

The incident of the 1962 book-defacing offence was also dredged up. After the court trial of 1962 both Orton and Halliwell had been sentenced to six months' imprisonment but the public was outraged – not by the severity of the sentence, but by its lenity.

One commentator said: 'People who deface library books must be dead to all sense of shame; six months' imprisonment, the severest sentence that the law allowed, is totally inadequate for a crime of that kind.'

Yet how strange is the world that over thirty years later Islington Library – the very library that instituted the prosecution against Orton and Halliwell – could proudly proclaim that an exhibition of the books defaced was to be held. Anyone wanting to visit the exhibition and see the images that outraged an earlier generation now had to pay an entrance fee. The defaced books – showing among other things Winston Churchill's head on an ape – had become enormously valuable and still are. They are now among the library's most prized possessions. If Orton had never become famous the books no doubt would have been thrown away long ago – such is the extraordinary power of celebrity.

DEATH BY PELICAN

2006

There have been pelicans on the lake at St James's Park since the first few were presented to Charles II by the Czar of Russia in 1660. Nothing so exotic had ever been seen in the capital and Londoners flocked to the park to see the new arrivals.

By the early 1970s disease and bad luck had reduced the St James's flock of pelicans to just one bird. Something had to be done and with a sense of tradition typical of the Court of St James, it was recalled that the original birds had been presented by the Imperial Russian Court.

Despite the Cold War the British Government approached the Russian Government and asked if they could spare a few more birds. When the birds arrived everyone was delighted – except the other birds in the park.

The newspapers were filled with stories of songbirds and more especially pigeons being eaten by the pelicans – the stories were not generally believed because pelicans are not carnivores, but the experts had not reckoned on these new and very ferocious Communist pelicans. Proof was difficult to obtain until in 2006 a photographer managed to get a close-up picture of a plump woodpigeon disappearing into a pelican's gaping maw!

GOING DUTCH

2007

Dutch ships that land their cargoes in the City of London – admittedly a rare event today when most cargo is unloaded miles downriver at Tilbury – are never charged harbour fees.

In fact they have paid no fees since the plague year of 1665 when London was virtually cut off from the rest of the world.

No other nation would land its cargoes at that time for fear of catching the terrible disease; only the Dutch kept trading with London, dropping supplies of food and other goods vital to the survival of a city which has shown its gratitude ever since by waiving the charges that apply to all other nations.